NAUTICAL WONDERS

NAUTICAL WONDERS

Giants of Maritime Evolution

OLIVIA K

Spectra Enterprise

CONTENTS

Table of Content

Introduction

1. Introduction to the world's largest ships and their historical significance.
2. Exploration of early maritime achievements and the evolution of ship design.
3. Profiles of iconic vessels that paved the way for modern giants.

Chapter 1: Engineering Marvels Afloat
1.1 In-depth examination of the innovative technologies and engineering feats behind the construction of colossal
ships.
1.2 Exploration of materials, propulsion systems, and design principles that make these vessels extraordinary.
1.3 Specific engineering challenges and solutions.

Chapter 2: Giants on the Horizon
2.1 A journey through the timeline of significant maritime advancements.
2.2 Exploration of how the demand for larger and more specialized vessels evolved over time.
2.3 Highlighting key moments that marked a shift in the scale and capabilities of maritime giants.

Chapter 3: Masters of the Sea
3.1 Profiles of the world's largest ships, past and present.
3.2 Detailed narratives of their construction, maiden voyages, and notable accomplishments.
3.3 Insights into the roles these vessels play in various industries, from shipping to exploration.

Chapter 4: Conquering the Depths

4.1 Exploration of how modern maritime technology enables the construction of massive vessels capable of

navigating deep oceans.

4.2 Discussion of submersibles, submarines, and other cutting-edge technologies in the realm of underwater

exploration.

Chapter 5: Environmental Challenges and Solutions

5.1 Examination of the environmental impact of large ships.

5.2 Discussion of sustainable practices and technological innovations aimed at minimizing the ecological footprint

of maritime giants.

5.3 Eco-friendly initiatives within the maritime industry.

Chapter 6: Beyond Boundaries: Future Prospects

6.1 Speculation on the future of maritime evolution and the potential for even larger, more advanced vessels.

6.2 Exploration of emerging technologies, including automation, artificial intelligence, and alternative fuels.

6.3 Discussion on the implications of evolving maritime trends for global trade and exploration.

Chapter 7: Navigating the Unknown

7.1 Reflection on the overall impact of giants of maritime evolution on human society and the global economy.

7.2 Contemplation of the ongoing challenges and opportunities in the world of large ships.

7.3 Closing thoughts on the enduring legacy of these nautical wonders.

Introduction

The oceanic world has for quite some time been a venue of human inventiveness and investigation, with the journey for bigger and more impressive vessels remaining as a demonstration of our constant quest for progress. As we leave on an excursion through the chronicles of oceanic history, it becomes evident that the development of boat plan and development has been unpredictably woven into the texture of human progress. The world's biggest boats, frequently wonders of designing, stand as substantial images of our constant desire to vanquish the oceans.

In the early parts of sea history, vessels were unobtrusive in scale and fundamentally filled useful needs like transportation and exchange. These modest starting points, nonetheless, established the groundwork for the possible development of nautical goliaths. The verifiable account is rich with stories of investigation and marine undertakings, with vessels like the St Nick Maria and the Mayflower drawing their names into the annals of sea advancement. These trailblazers, however predominated by contemporary principles, set forth into unknown waters and prepared for the goliath delivers that would follow.

The change from wooden cruising boats to press and steel-hulled vessels denoted a critical defining moment in sea designing. The coming of steam power additionally reformed the capacities of boats, empowering them to explore with more noteworthy speed and effectiveness. The mid-nineteenth century saw the ascent of steamships, an innovative jump that foreshadowed the time of oceanic goliaths. The Incomparable Eastern, a behemoth of now is the right time, exemplified this progress, exhibiting the potential for bigger and all the more remarkable vessels.

As the twentieth century unfurled, the interest for bigger boats turned out to be more articulated, driven by the expanding needs of worldwide exchange and investigation. The Titanic, a grievous yet famous image of sea desire, addressed the zenith of extravagance and scale in its period. The boat, with its magnificence and mechanical complexity, epitomized the embodiment of oceanic accomplishment. However, the

Titanic's destiny additionally highlighted the dangers related with pushing the limits of sea designing.

In the last 50% of the twentieth 100 years and into the 21st hundred years, the sea business saw a renaissance in transport plan and development.

The rise of containerization and the remarkable development of global exchange powered the requirement for vessels equipped for moving huge amounts of merchandise across the seas. This request led to another type of monsters — holder ships and oil big haulers that overshadowed their ancestors. The Emma Maersk, one such holder transport, exemplified this pattern, flaunting gigantic aspects and limits beforehand incomprehensible.

The designing wonders that support these nautical goliaths are absolutely phenomenal. The shift from traditional propeller frameworks to creative impetus innovations, like podded drive and LNG motors, has upgraded the effectiveness and natural maintainability of these vessels. The utilization of cutting edge materials, including high-strength amalgams and composite designs, has took into account the development of bigger boats while keeping up with primary respectability. The complex dance between maritime design, materials science, and drive designing has pushed oceanic development to phenomenal levels.

Past the domains of freight transportation, oceanic goliaths have tracked down application in different areas. Journey ships, drifting urban communities of richness and diversion, have re-imagined the idea of extravagance travel. Maritime vessels, including plane carrying warships and submarines, epitomize the tactical uses of enormous boats, exhibiting their essential significance in worldwide international relations. Logical investigation has additionally profited from enormous examination vessels furnished with cutting edge labs, empowering scientists to dive into the secrets of the sea profundities.

As we wonder about the sheer size and capacities of these nautical marvels, taking into account the ecological ramifications of such enormous vessels is fundamental. The delivery business, liable for a huge part of worldwide fossil fuel byproducts, faces expanding examination and strain to take on manageable practices. Developments, for example, wind-helped impetus, elective powers, and emanation decrease innovations are becoming basic for the business' future. Finding some kind of harmony between financial objectives and natural stewardship is a test that the sea area should stand up to in the continuous excursion of oceanic development.

Looking forward, the fate of sea development holds both commitment and vulnerability. Arising advances, for example, independent vessels and man-made consciousness, stand ready to alter the manner in which we explore the oceans. The possibility of drifting sun based ranches and green delivery drives recommends a pathway toward a more economical sea future. In any case, difficulties like international strains, administrative intricacies, and the continuous mission for monetary productivity highlight the complexities of exploring the obscure waters that lie ahead.

The goliaths of sea advancement stand as living demonstrations of human development, desire, and the persistent craving to investigate the huge field of the world's seas. From humble starting points to the state of the art innovations of today, the excursion through oceanic history uncovers an adventure of wins, misfortunes, and the consistent journey for progress.

As we set forth into the future, the nautical marvels that spot the seascape act as guides of motivation, helping us that the development to remember oceanic designing is a continuous odyssey — one that impels humankind forward on the perpetual skyline of investigation.

1. **Introduction to the world's largest ships and their historical significance.**
   The tremendous territory of the world's seas has been both a jungle gym for investigation and a venue for exhibiting human resourcefulness as oceanic designing. At the very front of this sea development stand the world's biggest boats, monster vessels that push the limits of size, designing, and usefulness. As we dig into the verifiable meaning of these sea goliaths, we set out on an excursion through time, following the foundations of nautical marvels that play played significant parts in forming the course of mankind's set of experiences.
   The early parts of sea history uncover an unassuming starting set apart by wooden cruising ships exploring the oceans for exchange and investigation. These vessels, however unobtrusive in size contrasted with their advanced partners, established the groundwork for the development of boat plan. Any semblance of the St Nick Maria, Christopher Columbus' notorious leader, and the Mayflower, which conveyed the Travelers to the New World, set up for the oceanic undertakings that would follow. These vessels, while overshadowed by contemporary guidelines, represent the boldness of early sailors who wandered into the obscure with simple yet momentous innovation.
   The progress from wooden boats to press and steel-hulled vessels in the nineteenth century denoted a groundbreaking period in oceanic designing. Steam power arose as a unique advantage, impelling boats with recently discovered speed and productivity. The Incomparable Eastern, a huge vessel of now is the right time, exhibited the potential for bigger and all the more mechanically progressed ships. This period laid the basis for the fantastic changes in transport plan and development that would characterize the twentieth and 21st hundreds of years.
   The Titanic, a name carved into the records of oceanic history, addresses a urgent second in the mission for bigger and more lavish vessels. As an image of plushness and high level designing, the Titanic exemplified the goals of its period. Be that as it may, the appalling sinking of the Titanic additionally highlighted the dangers inborn in stretching the boundaries of oceanic innovation. In spite of the misfortune, the Titanic remaining parts a standard for understanding the crossing point of human desire and the difficulties presented by the

unusual powers of the ocean.

The last 50% of the twentieth century saw a change in perspective in the interest for bigger boats, driven by the globalization of exchange and the requirement for more productive transportation. Containerization upset the delivery business, leading to enormous compartment sends that could ship merchandise on a phenomenal scale. The Emma Maersk, one of the biggest holder delivers at any point constructed, represents this time of sea advancement. With its giant size and stunning freight limit, the Emma Maersk mirrors the changing elements of worldwide business.

The designing wonders that support the world's biggest boats are a demonstration of human development and innovative ability. From cutting edge impetus frameworks to state of the art materials, the development of these vessels includes an intricate exchange of science and designing. Advancements like podded impetus, LNG motors, and the utilization of high-strength combinations have raised the proficiency and abilities of these oceanic goliaths. The fastidious combination of maritime design, materials science, and impetus designing has moved the business to new boondocks.

Past the domain of freight transportation, oceanic goliaths have tracked down different applications. Journey ships, frequently alluded to as drifting urban communities, have re-imagined the idea of extravagance travel. These vessels, furnished with conveniences going from theaters to water parks, feature the convergence of oceanic designing and the neighborliness business. Maritime vessels, including plane carrying warships and submarines, exhibit the essential significance of epic boats in worldwide military activities. Furthermore, research vessels furnished with best in class labs assume a vital part in progressing logical investigation of the seas.

While the world's biggest boats address surprising accomplishments of designing, they likewise raise ecological contemplations. The delivery business, liable for a critical piece of worldwide fossil fuel byproducts, faces expanding strain to take on economical practices. Drives, for example, wind-helped impetus, elective fills, and emanation decrease advancements are becoming basic for the business' drawn out reasonability. Finding some kind of harmony between monetary goals and ecological obligation represents a test that the sea area should face as it outlines the course for what's to come.

Looking forward, the fate of sea advancement holds both commitment and vulnerability. Arising innovations, including independent vessels and man-made reasoning, can possibly alter the manner in which we explore the oceans. The possibility of drifting sun based homesteads and green delivery drives proposes a pathway toward a more feasible sea future. Notwithstanding, difficulties like international pressures, administrative intricacies, and the continuous journey for monetary proficiency highlight the intricacies of exploring the obscure waters that lie ahead.

The world's biggest boats stand as stupendous accomplishments in the continuous adventure of oceanic development. From the beginning of wooden cruising boats to the state of the art advancements of today, these nautical marvels mirror the dauntless soul of human investigation and development. As we consider their authentic importance, we perceive that the advancement of sea designing is a perplexing embroidery woven with wins, misfortunes, and the unending quest for progress. The world's seas, crossed by these enormous vessels, keep on being a material whereupon humankind writes its mission for information, experience, and the tenacious quest for skylines yet to be investigated.

2. **Exploration of early maritime achievements and the evolution of ship design.**

The embroidery of sea history unfurls with a rich exhibit of early accomplishments, each string adding to the development of boat plan and the investigation of unfamiliar waters. In the archives of time, the tradition of early sea attempts is woven into the texture of human progress, uncovering the daringness of sailors who tried to vanquish the endlessness of the world's seas.

The underlying foundations of sea investigation expand profound into vestige, with old civilizations wandering past beach front waters for exchange, investigation, and triumph. The Phoenicians, known for their sea ability, explored the Mediterranean Ocean, laying out shipping lanes and settlements that laid the foundation for interconnected marine societies. The Greeks, as well, wandered into the Aegean and then some, presenting headways in transport plan and route methods.

The improvement of boat plan in days of yore was set apart by the development from straightforward wooden vessels to more refined cruising ships. The warship, a warship with three banks of paddles, turned into a notable image of maritime power in the old world. Its plan, portrayed by a smooth structure and various lines of paddles, displayed the combination of reasonableness and development in early shipbuilding.

The Vikings, nautical Norse individuals from the late eighth to mid eleventh hundred years, are unbelievable figures in sea history. Their longships, with their shallow draft and adaptable plan, permitted them to explore both untamed oceans and shallow waterways. The Viking longship's notorious outline, embellished with a mythical beast's head fore, stays a getting through image of early maritime ability.

As human advancements extended and shipping lanes thrived, the requirement for bigger and more flexible vessels became evident. The Time of Investigation in the fifteenth and sixteenth hundreds of years saw a flood in sea movement prodded by the longing to lay out new shipping lanes and find unfamiliar grounds. Christopher Columbus' journeys to the Americas, worked with by the Spanish Crown, denoted a defining moment in sea history.

The caravel, a little and flexibility transport with a particular three-sided lateen sail, became inseparable from these early transoceanic campaigns.

In the seventeenth 100 years, the Dutch East India Organization assumed a urgent part in oceanic exchange, utilizing huge and vigorously furnished trader ships known as East Indiamen. These vessels, intended for both exchange and protection, exemplified the combination of trade and maritime capacity. The period likewise saw the development of shipbuilding methods that integrated iron into body development, upgrading the toughness and fitness for sailing of vessels.

The eighteenth century introduced the time of sail, described by glorious tall boats with transcending poles and surging sails. The plan and development of these boats arrived at new levels of refinement, with headways in gear, route, and maritime engineering. The Imperial Naval force's HMS Triumph, a top notch boat of the line, remains as a demonstration of the magnificence and intricacy of eighteenth century transport plan.

The progress from sail to steam in the nineteenth century denoted a progressive period in sea history. Steamships, impelled by steam motors, changed the elements of maritime fighting and business. The SS Extraordinary England, sent off in 1843, was a spearheading steamship planned by Isambard Realm Brunel. With an iron frame and a screw propeller, the SS Extraordinary England joined the developments of the Modern Unrest with sea designing, starting a trend for what's to come.

The approach of iron and steel-hulled ships in the late nineteenth century further upset transport plan. The CSS Virginia and the USS Screen, iron-clad warships from the American Nationwide conflict, exhibited the strength of metal-hulled vessels in maritime clash. The change from sail to steam and the fuse of metal into transport development established the groundwork for the improvement of the epic vessels that would overwhelm the oceans in the twentieth 100 years.

The mid twentieth century saw the brilliant period of sea liners, embodied by vessels like the RMS Titanic. These extravagance liners, set apart by lavish insides and high level designing, represented the level of class in oceanic travel. The Titanic, with its sheer size and mechanical refinement, turned into a heartbreaking yet notable portrayal of the desires and difficulties of the time.

The development of boat configuration proceeded with unabated during the twentieth hundred years with the approach of containerization. The compartment transport, for example, the Ocean Land holder transport, presented normalized freight holders that altered the productivity of freight transportation. This advancement changed the transportation business as well as impacted port framework and worldwide exchange designs.

The last 50% of the twentieth hundred years and the mid 21st century saw the ascent of super big haulers, holder uber ships, and enormous luxury ships. The Seawise Goliath, later known as the Jahre Viking, held the title of the biggest boat at any point fabricated, displaying the sheer scale that oceanic designing had accomplished. Holder ships like the Emma Maersk set new norms for freight limit, mirroring the dramatic development in worldwide exchange.

The investigation of early sea accomplishments and the development of boat configuration is a demonstration of the dauntless human soul. From the humble vessels of antiquated human advancements to the huge boats of the cutting edge period, every section in sea history mirrors the desires, difficulties, and developments of now is the right time. As we explore the waters of the past, we gain a significant appreciation for the sailors and shipbuilders who, with resourcefulness and assurance, molded the course of sea development.

3. **Profiles of iconic vessels that paved the way for modern giants.**

In the excellent embroidered artwork of oceanic history, certain vessels stand apart as trailblazers, establishing the groundwork for the cutting edge goliaths that would later rule the oceans. These notable boats, with their earth shattering plans and noteworthy journeys, have made a permanent imprint on the advancement of sea designing.

One such incredible vessel is the St Nick Maria, the lead of Christopher Columbus' 1492 campaign to the Americas. A carrack, a sort of enormous cruising transport, the St Nick Maria addressed the zenith of fifteenth century sea innovation. Its plan included a high forecastle and sterncastle, giving a competitive edge to protection and route. While not especially enormous by contemporary guidelines, the St Nick Maria's part in Columbus' memorable excursion marks it as a pioneer in the period of investigation.

Quick forward to the seventeenth 100 years, and the Dutch East India Organization's Batavia arises as another sea pioneer. A Dutch East Indiaman, the Batavia was a huge, vigorously equipped dealer transport intended for significant distance journeys toward the East Indies. With its strong structure and strong deadly implement, the Batavia exemplified the combination of exchange and guard in oceanic undertakings. This double reason configuration set up for the later development of half breed vessels that could explore deceptive waters while guaranteeing the wellbeing of important freight.

The HMS Triumph, a top notch boat of the line sent off in 1765, is an image of maritime ability during the period of sail. As the leader of Chief naval officer Horatio Nelson at the Clash of Trafalgar, the Triumph assumed an unequivocal part in getting English maritime matchless quality. With its three weapon decks and transcending poles, the Triumph addressed the pinnacle of wooden boat plan. Its many-sided fixing and painstakingly determined balance made it a considerable power on the high oceans, impacting maritime design for a long time into the future.

The change from sail to steam in the nineteenth century delivered the SS Extraordinary England, a spearheading steamship planned by Isambard Realm Brunel. Sent off in 1843, the SS Extraordinary England was the principal iron-hulled, screw-impelled sea liner. Brunel's inventive plan integrated a blend of an iron body, a screw propeller, and a steam motor, reforming sea innovation. The boat's overseas journeys denoted a defining moment in the practicality of steam-fueled sea travel, making ready for the period of steamships.

The CSS Virginia and the USS Screen, ironclad warships from the American Nationwide conflict, address an essential second in maritime fighting and boat plan. The CSS Virginia, worked by the Confederate Naval force, included an iron-clad body and a steam-controlled motor. Its Association partner, the USS Screen, was the main ironclad warship dispatched by the US Naval force. The conflict between these two ironclads at the Skirmish of Hampton Streets in 1862 denoted the start of another time in maritime fighting, as customary wooden warships became old.

The RMS Titanic, sent off in 1912, is maybe the most notorious and awful vessel in oceanic history. Planned as the encapsulation of extravagance, the Titanic was the biggest and most developed sea liner of now is the ideal time. With its great insides, high level wellbeing highlights, and sheer size, the Titanic caught the world's creative mind. Be that as it may, the boat's doomed first trip, finishing off with catastrophe with the ice shelf crash, featured the weakness of even the most innovatively progressed vessels. The Titanic's inheritance is one of both victory and misfortune, molding sea wellbeing guidelines for a long time into the future.

The SS Normandie, a French sea liner sent off in 1935, addressed the exemplification of craftsmanship deco style and sea extravagance. With its smooth plan, imaginative body shape, and luxurious insides, the Normandie set new guidelines for overseas travel. Notwithstanding its generally short vocation and heartbreaking end in a fire at a New York City wharf in 1942, the Normandie's effect on transport plan and feel persevered, impacting resulting ages of sea liners.

The USS Nautilus, the world's most memorable functional atomic fueled submarine, represents an upset in submerged investigation and fighting. Sent off in 1954, the Nautilus presented atomic impetus, offering stretched out range and the capacity to work lowered for delayed periods. This innovative jump reshaped maritime system and impacted the plan of resulting atomic controlled submarines, making ready for another period of undersea investigation and safeguard.

The presentation of containerization during the twentieth century delivered the Ocean Land holder transport, a vessel that assumed a vital part in upsetting worldwide exchange. The Ocean Land Vessel, sent off in 1956, was the world's most memorable compartment transport intended for the effective vehicle of normalized freight holders. This creative way to deal with freight taking care of changed port activities, coordinated operations, and the financial aspects of transportation, making way for the compartment uber boats of the 21st 100 years.

The Sovereign Elizabeth 2 (QE2), sent off in 1967, is a famous sea liner that turned into an image of English sea custom. With its unmistakable pipe and exemplary plan, the QE2 consolidated extravagance with usefulness. All through its profession, the

QE2 filled in as both an overseas liner and a journey transport, displaying the versatility of sea designing to changing patterns in movement and the travel industry.

In the domain of logical investigation, the examination vessel Calypso, captained by Jacques Cousteau, stands apart as a spearheading vessel. Initially an English Imperial Naval force minesweeper, Cousteau changed over the Calypso into an exploration vessel prepared for oceanographic endeavors. The vessel assumed an essential part in propelling sea life science and submerged filmmaking, bringing the marvels of the sea profundities to the worldwide crowd.

As we consider these profiles of notable vessels, a consistent idea arises — each boat addresses an achievement in oceanic history, pushing the limits of plan, innovation, and investigation. From the wooden structures of the St Nick Maria to the atomic controlled drive of the USS Nautilus, these vessels have on the whole molded the direction of sea development, passing on a getting through inheritance that keeps on affecting the boats that beauty the oceans today.

The Seawise Monster, later known as the Jahre Viking, holds an unmistakable spot in the pantheon of sea goliaths. Sent off in 1979, this supertanker turned into the biggest boat at any point developed, bragging a length 458 meters (1,504 feet) and an extra weight of more than 564,000 tons when completely stacked. The Seawise Monster addressed a zenith in the designing and development of enormous vessels, underlining the job of these goliaths in the transportation of oil and different products on a worldwide scale.

Holder ships, like the Emma Maersk, have re-imagined the scene of sea business in the 21st 100 years. Sent off in 2006, the Emma Maersk set new standards as the biggest compartment transport at that point. With a length surpassing 397 meters (1,302 feet) and a limit of north of 15,000 twenty-foot comparable units (TEUs), it represents the productivity and scale requested by the cutting edge transporting industry. These compartment super ships have turned into the foundation of worldwide exchange, working with the development of products between mainlands with unrivaled effectiveness.

Journey sends, the drifting urban communities of the oceans, have seen a striking development in size and extravagance. The Orchestra of the Oceans, sent off in 2018, is right now the world's biggest journey transport. With a length of 362 meters (1,188 feet) and a limit of more than 6,600 travelers, it offers a stunning exhibit of conveniences, including theaters, water parks, and a Focal Park-themed promenade. These advanced luxury ships represent the convergence of sea designing and the cordiality business, giving travelers an unmatched involvement with ocean.

In the domain of maritime power, plane carrying warships have turned into the encapsulation of oceanic strength and projection. The USS Gerald R. Passage, charged in 2017, is the lead boat of the US Naval force's Portage class of plane carrying warships. With a general length of 337 meters (1,106 feet) and a relocation of more than 100,000 tons, it addresses the most recent headways in maritime innovation. Including electromagnetic slings for airplane send off and an upgraded flight deck, the USS

Gerald R. Portage features the continuous advancement of maritime vessels that act as versatile airbases and power projection stages.

The Almirante Irízar, an Argentine icebreaker, gives a brief look into the specific vessels intended for polar investigation. Initially sent off in 1978, the Almirante Irízar went through broad modernization and repair, displaying the flexibility and life span of specific sea vessels. Prepared to explore through ice-shrouded waters, icebreakers assume a pivotal part in working with polar examination and guaranteeing safe entry through Cold and Antarctic locales.

As we ponder these advanced goliaths, it becomes obvious that their jobs reach out past business and investigation. They represent the innovative ability of the countries that build them, the monetary reliance cultivated by worldwide exchange, and the essential meaning of oceanic power. Also, these vessels highlight the persistent mission for effectiveness, security, and supportability in oceanic designing, as the business wrestles with natural difficulties and makes progress toward creative arrangements.

The profiles of notable vessels crossing hundreds of years uncover a sensational excursion of sea advancement. From the humble yet trying St Nick Maria to the monster Seawise Goliath, each boat has made a permanent imprint on history, forming the course of sea designing and investigation. These vessels stand as demonstration of human creativity, versatility, and the perpetual quest for progress on the world's seas. As we explore the oceans representing things to come, the tradition of these sea goliaths keeps on motivating the up and coming age of architects, mariners, and wayfarers, alluring them to outline new skylines and push the limits of what is considered conceivable on the huge and dynamic material of the world's waters.

Chapter 1

Engineering Marvels Afloat

Designing Wonders Above water: An Excursion Through Nautical Creativity
In the tremendous domain of sea designing, where the powers of nature and the requests of human investigation merge, a staggering embroidery of development unfurls. "Designing Wonders Above water" is a complete investigation of the historic headways that have formed the universe of boats and nautical. From antiquated sea developments to the state of the art advances of the current day, this excursion through nautical resourcefulness traverses the profundities of history and the boundlessness of the untamed ocean.

The odyssey starts with a reflection on the earliest indications of sea designing — the crude yet shrewd vessels made by old developments. Whether it be the tough reed boats of the antiquated Egyptians or the smooth warships of the Greeks, these early sailors established the groundwork for the development of sea designing. Through experimentation, they excelled at boatbuilding, opening the potential for human investigation across seas and streams.

As the story sails through time, the center movements to the time of investigation, a period set apart by the fearless excursions of pilots and mariners looking for new skylines. The display enlightens the plan standards and navigational procedures utilized in the development of famous vessels, for example, the caravels and ships.

These boats, with their unmistakable sails and frames, turned into the vehicles of revelation, impelling adventurers like Christopher Columbus and Ferdinand Magellan into strange waters.

The progress from wind-fueled vessels to the period of steam power is a crucial section in sea history. The persevering quest for proficiency and speed prompted the improvement of steam motors, altering maritime design. The trimmers, with their smooth lines and transcending poles, address the encapsulation of nineteenth century designing ability. Guests to the show can wonder about fastidiously created models, each a demonstration of the combination of workmanship and designing that characterized this brilliant time of sail.

The coming of the twentieth century introduced another time of sea designing described by gigantic sea liners and imposing war vessels. The display gives a vivid encounter, permitting guests to step on board scaled imitations of extravagance liners like the Titanic or investigate the complicated insides of maritime warships. The designing difficulties presented by these goliaths of the ocean, from drive frameworks to underlying respectability, are rejuvenated through intuitive showcases and interactive media introductions.

Submarines, the quiet sentinels of the profound, become the overwhelming focus in the story as the show dives into the world underneath the sea's surface. From early hand-wrenched submarines to the atomic fueled behemoths of the Virus War, the development of submarine innovation is a demonstration of human advancement notwithstanding misfortune. Guests can dive into the confined quarters of a submarine or witness the complexities of sonar and route frameworks that empower these vessels to explore concealed and unheard.

The presentation's investigation of contemporary oceanic designing features the continuous quest for independence and supportability. Independent vessels furnished with cutting edge route frameworks and man-made reasoning are displayed as harbingers representing things to come. The fragile harmony between mechanical headway and natural obligation is exemplified through reasonable boat plans that focus on effectiveness and limit environmental effect.

A section on shipbuilding strategies offers an in the background take a gander at the craftsmanship and accuracy expected to build current vessels. From the choice of materials to the complexities of welding and forming, the designing wonders above water today are the consequence of an amicable mix of custom and state of the art innovation.

Proceeding with our excursion through the chronicles of sea history, the narrative of designing wonders above water would be deficient without a more intensive glance at the complexities of boat plan and the interesting stories of mechanical forward leaps that have molded nautical developments.

Transport plan, a basic feature of sea designing, has developed over hundreds of years, adjusting to evolving needs, innovative progressions, and the intrinsic difficulties of the ocean. The progress from wooden cruising boats to press and steel bodies denoted a huge jump forward in shipbuilding. Iron-hulled ships offered expanded strength and diminished upkeep, proclaiming another time of sea engineering. This shift improved the life span of vessels as well as prepared for the development of bigger, stronger boats equipped for enduring the afflictions of the untamed sea.

The Modern Unrest achieved extraordinary changes in shipbuilding strategies. The coming of steam power prompted the development of steamships, adjusting the elements of oceanic travel. The use of paddlewheels and later the improvement of propellers changed the impetus frameworks of boats, upgrading their speed and mobility.

Ironclad warships arose, including reinforced bodies that changed maritime fighting. The USS Screen and the CSS Virginia, well known ironclads from the American Nationwide conflict, embody this time of development in maritime plan.

The late nineteenth century saw the union of steam and sail, bringing about mixture vessels that consolidated the unwavering quality of steam power with the adaptability of conventional sails. These mixture ships, like the tea trimmers and early steamships, exemplified a momentary stage in oceanic designing, exhibiting the concurrence of old and new advances as the business adjusted to the evolving times.

The twentieth century delivered uncommon headways in maritime engineering, especially in the domain of impetus. The change from coal-terminated motors to oil-terminated motors denoted an essential second, smoothing out tasks and expanding the proficiency of marine impetus frameworks. The improvement of diesel motors additionally refined sea innovation, offering a more eco-friendly choice to steam power. These developments impacted business delivery as well as assumed a pivotal part in the rise of strong maritime armadas during seasons of worldwide struggle.

The Second Great War and The Second Great War prodded quick progressions in maritime designing, leading to famous vessels that made a permanent imprint on oceanic history. The ship, when the highlight of maritime power, developed into considerable conflict machines furnished with cutting edge weaponry and radar frameworks. Plane carrying warships, a progressive idea that reclassified maritime fighting, became drifting airbases fit for extending power across immense scopes of sea.

Submarines, at first created for subtle observation, arose as intense hostile weapons. The coming of atomic drive slung submarines into another time of perseverance and vital capacity. The Virus War saw a race between superpowers to construct bigger, calmer, and further developed submarines, prompting the improvement of atomic fueled long range rocket submarines (SSBNs) that assumed a pivotal part in prevention methodologies.

As the show advances into the last 50% of the twentieth hundred years, the center movements to the space race and its effect on oceanic innovation. Satellite route frameworks, at first produced for space investigation, tracked down applications in sea route, altogether upgrading the accuracy and unwavering quality of boat situating. The coordination of satellite correspondence frameworks altered sea tasks, empowering constant correspondence among boats and shores.

The last option part of the twentieth 100 years and the mid 21st century saw a change in outlook in sea innovation with the development of containerization. Compartment ships, intended to convey normalized freight holders, smoothed out the worldwide delivery industry, radically decreasing stacking and dumping times and expanding the productivity of freight transport. This advancement worked with the globalization of exchange, associating far off ports and markets in a complicated snare of oceanic business.

The contemporary time of oceanic designing is portrayed by a persistent quest for independence and manageability. Independent vessels, directed by man-made brainpower and modern sensor frameworks, address the outskirts of oceanic investigation. These automated boats, fit for exploring immense distances without human mediation, hold the commitment of changing the scene of delivery and sea investigation.

Maintainability is a main impetus in current boat plan, with an emphasis on eco-accommodating drive frameworks, energy-productive advances, and earth cognizant practices. The improvement of wind-help innovations, for example, sails and rotor sails, plans to bridle environmentally friendly power sources and diminish the carbon impression of sea transportation. Moreover, headways in body plan and coatings endeavor to limit the ecological effect of vessels on marine environments.

"Designing Wonders Above water" unfurls as an arresting narrative of human resourcefulness and mechanical development on the high oceans. From the unobtrusive boats of old sailors to the independent vessels representing things to come, every part in sea history mirrors the persistence of the human soul to overcome the difficulties presented by the tremendous and flighty sea. As guests stroll through the display, they are submerged in a story that commends the convergence of development, investigation, and designing greatness — a demonstration of the persevering through tradition of the people who have really considered exploring the world's waters in quest for disclosure and progress.

1.1 In-depth examination of the innovative technologies and engineering feats behind the construction of colossal ships.

The development of goliath ships addresses a zenith of sea designing, mixing state of the art innovations with revered standards to make vessels that push the limits of size, usefulness, and effectiveness.

This top to bottom assessment dives into the creative advances and designing accomplishments that support the development of these maritime monsters, giving experiences into the intricacies engaged with rejuvenating these goliath structures.

One of the basic parts of boat development lies in the materials utilized. Conventional materials like wood have given way to additional powerful and adaptable materials, like steel and aluminum. These metals offer predominant strength and toughness, urgent for vessels that face the unforgiving and destructive conditions of the vast ocean. The appearance of high-strength compounds has additionally improved the primary respectability of boat structures, considering the formation of bigger and stronger vessels.

The development interaction itself is a fastidiously organized artful dance of designing accuracy. Shipbuilding includes a grouping of stages, starting with the plan stage. Maritime draftsmen use progressed PC supported plan (computer aided design) programming to demonstrate and mimic each part of a boat's construction, from its frame structure to its interior compartments. This advanced displaying considers the improvement of boat plans, guaranteeing effectiveness in execution, security, and fuel utilization.

When the plan is concluded, the real development starts with the laying of the fall — the foundation of the boat. Shipbuilders utilize complex welding strategies to collect the fall and edge, framing the skeleton of the vessel. The development of goliath transports frequently includes secluded development, where various segments of the boat, known as blocks, are manufactured independently and afterward collected. This particular methodology smoothes out the development cycle, empowering concurrent work on numerous segments.

The structure, a basic part of any boat, goes through fastidious consideration. Shipbuilders utilize creative welding strategies, including automated welding for accuracy and productivity, to guarantee the underlying respectability of the frame. What's more, hostile to erosion coatings and cathodic insurance frameworks are coordinated into the body plan to defend against the destructive impacts of seawater.

The impetus framework is a vital concentration in the designing of titanic boats. While conventional boats depended on sails or steam motors, current vessels frequently highlight modern drive frameworks, including diesel-electric, gas turbine, or even atomic impetus. The decision of impetus relies upon the planned utilization of the boat, whether it be for business transportation, maritime tasks, or logical exploration. Progresses in impetus innovation mean to amplify eco-friendliness, diminish emanations, and improve generally execution.

The mix of cutting edge route and control frameworks is vital in guaranteeing the security and mobility of enormous boats.

Worldwide Situating Framework (GPS) innovation, gyrators, and high level radar frameworks empower exact route, permitting boats to cross many-sided courses with precision. Computerization assumes an essential part in current boat control, with modernized frameworks overseeing drive, route, and even crash evasion. These mechanical progressions upgrade security as well as add to the functional effectiveness of monster vessels.

In the domain of boat insides, the designing center stretches out past underlying components to envelop the enhancement of living and working spaces. Giant boats, whether luxury ships or maritime vessels, are intended to oblige huge teams or travelers for broadened periods. Ergonomics, proficient space usage, and contemplations for solace and security are central. Developments in inside plan incorporate particular living quarters, energy-effective lighting and environment control frameworks, and high level waste administration answers for guarantee an economical and tenable climate ready.

The designing wonders of epic boats stretch out to the domain of energy proficiency and natural supportability. The sea business faces expanding strain to lessen its ecological effect, provoking the coordination of green advances in transport plan. Energy-productive impetus frameworks, for example, slow-steaming to advance fuel utilization, and the investigation of elective powers like melted flammable gas (LNG) add to decreasing ozone depleting substance emanations. Furthermore, developments in body configuration, for example, air grease frameworks and high level coatings, mean to limit frictional obstruction and upgrade eco-friendliness.

Wellbeing is a vital worry in oceanic designing, particularly for enormous boats that convey huge quantities of travelers or significant freight. High level security highlights incorporate best in class fire concealment frameworks, crisis departure strategies, and state of the art route helps. The consolidation of repetitive frameworks and safeguard components guarantees that gigantic boats can endure unexpected difficulties, from antagonistic weather patterns to mechanical disappointments.

The development of goliath ships isn't restricted to the actual vessels yet stretches out to the improvement of particular framework to help their activities. Seaports and terminals are designed to oblige the size and draft of these gigantic vessels, with profound billets, high level freight taking care of gear, and cutting edge security frameworks. The joining of shrewd port innovations, including computerized cranes and advanced coordinated factors stages, upgrades the effectiveness of stacking and dumping activities.

As gigantic boats set forth, they face the continuous test of support and fixes in the brutal marine climate. Dry docks, offices intended to oblige the docking and over-hauling of enormous vessels, assume a pivotal part in this part of sea designing.

Epic boats might require occasional dry-mooring for investigations, frame cleaning, and support assignments. Trend setting innovations, like remotely worked submerged vehicles (ROVs) and submerged welding methods, work with in-water upkeep to limit free time.

The ecological effect of enormous boats has turned into a point of convergence in oceanic designing. The business is investigating creative answers for moderate the environmental impression of delivery. Counterbalance water treatment frameworks forestall the spread of obtrusive species, and waste administration advancements guarantee capable removal of sewage and other waste. Furthermore, research is in progress to foster zero-discharge impetus frameworks, for example, hydrogen energy components and battery-electric innovations, to introduce another period of harmless to the ecosystem sea transportation.

The development of epic boats remains as a demonstration of the constant quest for development and designing greatness in the oceanic business. From the underlying plan stage to the coordination of best in class impetus frameworks, security highlights, and ecological manageability measures, goliath ships epitomize the finish of hundreds of years of sea designing advancement. These vessels, whether serving business, mili-tary, or logical purposes, explore the oceans as images of human creativity, pushing the limits of what is conceivable on the tremendous and dynamic material of the world's seas.

1.2 Exploration of materials, propulsion systems, and design principles that make these vessels extraordinary.

Leaving on an inside and out investigation of titanic boats divulges a captivating excursion through the perplexing trap of materials, drive frameworks, and plan rules that on the whole change these vessels into remarkable accomplishments of designing. From the sub-atomic organization of their bodies to the drive frameworks that impel them across the untamed ocean, enormous boats address an amicable combination of development, accuracy, and usefulness.

The underpinning of any boat lies in the materials that comprise its design, and for titanic boats, the determination of materials is a principal thought. Customarily, ships were made from wood, a material famous for its lightness and usefulness. Notwithstanding, as the requests of sea investigation advanced, so too did the materials utilized in transport development. The shift from wood to metals, explicitly steel and aluminum, denoted a turning point in oceanic designing.

Steel, with its prevalent strength, solidness, and protection from consumption, arose as the material of decision for building the frames of huge boats. The capacity to endure the tireless attack of saltwater and the difficulties presented by the marine climate made steel a crucial part in current shipbuilding. The utilization of high-strength compounds additionally raised the primary respectability of gigantic boat structures, permitting them to explore the turbulent oceans with unrivaled flexibility.

Aluminum, valued for its lightweight properties and erosion opposition, tracked down its specialty in specific areas of boat development. While not generally so universal as steel in gigantic boat bodies, aluminum is in many cases utilized in unambiguous parts, like superstructures and lightweight segments, adding to by and large weight decrease and further developed eco-friendliness.

The development cycle of epic boats is an unpredictable dance of accuracy and scale. The plan stage makes way for the whole development process, with maritime engineers utilizing modern PC supported plan (computer aided design) programming to demonstrate and recreate each part of the vessel. These advanced models act as outlines for shipbuilders, directing them in the creation of every part with demanding accuracy.

When the plan is finished, the development starts with the laying of the fall — the foundation of the boat. Shipbuilders utilize progressed welding strategies to gather the fall and casing, making the skeletal construction whereupon the whole vessel will be assembled. Goliath delivers frequently go through particular development, where various segments, or blocks, are manufactured freely prior to being gathered. This particular methodology improves proficiency, taking into account simultaneous work on various areas and facilitating the general development timetable.

The structure, a basic component in transport configuration, goes through fastidious consideration during development. The welding of the body is an exact cycle, requesting precision to guarantee the primary uprightness of the vessel. Computerized welding frameworks and mechanical advancements have become basic in this stage, offering upgraded accuracy and proficiency. The frame isn't only a defensive shell yet a painstakingly created structure that impacts the boat's hydrodynamics, soundness, and in general execution.

Against erosion measures are coordinated into the development cycle to shield huge boat structures from the destructive impacts of seawater. Defensive coatings and cathodic insurance frameworks make a boundary against consumption, drawing out the life expectancy of the vessel. The thorough designing applied to body development guarantees that giant boats can endure the tenacious powers of the untamed sea, giving a steady stage to their sweeping processes.

Drive frameworks address the thumping heart of titanic boats, directing their presentation, productivity, and mobility. The advancement of drive innovation reflects the more extensive direction of sea designing, with every time presenting developments that reclassify the abilities of these maritime behemoths.

Conventional cruising ships depended on the force of the breeze to impel them across the oceans. The tastefulness of surging sails and the authority of route portrayed this well established technique for drive.

Be that as it may, as the requests for speed and unwavering quality expanded, the sea world went through a groundbreaking movement with the coming of steam power.

Steam motors, bridled during the modern unrest, upset oceanic transportation. Steamships, outfitted with paddlewheels or propellers, supplanted the dependence on wind and muscle power. This obvious a significant crossroads in sea history, empowering vessels to explore all the more reliably and typically, unbound by the impulses of weather conditions.

As the twentieth century unfurled, monster ships saw the reconciliation of more refined impetus frameworks. The progress from coal-terminated motors to oil-terminated motors denoted a critical jump forward. Diesel motors arose as predominant players, offering upgraded eco-friendliness, dependability, and reach. The capacity to convey bigger amounts of fuel permitted boats to cross longer distances without successive refueling quits, adding to the worldwide extension of oceanic shipping lanes.

Gas turbine drive frameworks further raised the capacities of titanic boats, especially in maritime vessels and rapid ships. The minimal and lightweight nature of gas turbines made them ideal for applications where space and weight were basic contemplations. The blend of gas turbines with conventional diesel motors in a CODAG (Joined Diesel and Gas) setup turned into a typical methodology, giving adaptability in improving effectiveness and speed.

The last option some portion of the twentieth century saw the coming of atomic impetus, an extraordinary innovation that reformed maritime vessels. Atomic controlled ships, for example, plane carrying warships and submarines, offered broadened functional reaches and the capacity to stay adrift for delayed periods without refueling. The sheer power created by atomic reactors pushed these vessels with unparalleled speed and perseverance, reshaping the elements of maritime fighting.

In the domain of contemporary gigantic boats, impetus frameworks keep on advancing to satisfy the needs of effectiveness and ecological supportability. The oceanic business faces expanding strain to lessen its carbon impression, provoking the investigation of elective fills and green innovations. Condensed Gaseous petrol (LNG) has arisen as a cleaner elective, diminishing discharges contrasted with customary non-renewable energy sources. Furthermore, the investigation of hydrogen power modules and battery-electric impetus frameworks holds guarantee for a future where gigantic boats can explore with insignificant ecological effect.

Plan standards assume a critical part in changing enormous boats from practical vessels into tasteful and effective wonders. Maritime planners explore a sensitive harmony among structure and capability, coordinating inventive plan components that upgrade both the presentation and visual allure of these maritime goliaths.

Hydrodynamics, the investigation of how water collaborates with the structure of a boat, directs the forming of gigantic boat plans. The objective is to limit opposition and enhance the vessel's presentation through different plan highlights, for example, bulbous quits body structures. Computational Liquid Elements (CFD) recreations empower maritime draftsmen to dissect and refine plans, guaranteeing ideal hydrodynamic productivity.

The game plan of inner spaces is a basic part of boat plan, particularly for giant ships that might oblige huge quantities of travelers or house broad freight. Ergonomics, the study of planning spaces for human use, impacts the design of living quarters, mutual regions, and work areas. The effective usage of room, joined with contemplations for solace and wellbeing, upgrades the general livability of titanic boats.

In the domain of maritime design, the superstructure of giant boats addresses a material for both usefulness and feel. The superstructure houses navigational gear, control focuses, and, on account of luxury ships, conveniences for travelers. Structural development in superstructure configuration means to make outwardly striking profiles while upgrading the appropriation of weight and keeping up with strength.

The combination of trend setting innovations stretches out past impetus and route to incorporate brilliant frameworks that upgrade the functional productivity and security of titanic boats. Computerization and network are key components of present day transport plan, with advanced innovations overseeing different parts of boat activities. Coordinated span frameworks, consolidating radar, GPS, and specialized devices, give an exhaustive perspective on the boat's environmental elements, supporting route and impact evasion.

Gigantic boats intended for traveler solace integrate a variety of conveniences and diversion choices. Luxury ships, specifically, are designed to give a consistent mix of extravagance, diversion, and culinary encounters. The building design, inside plan, and sporting offices all add to the general insight for travelers, changing titanic boats into drifting urban areas of recreation.

The journey for energy effectiveness and supportability impacts plan standards in contemporary shipbuilding. Developments in body configuration, for example, air oil frameworks, look to diminish frictional opposition and further develop eco-friendliness. The investigation of elective materials, for example, composites and light-weight compounds, adds to weight decrease and upgraded energy execution.

Wellbeing contemplations penetrate each part of monster transport plan. The execution of excess frameworks and safeguard instruments guarantees that these vessels can endure unexpected difficulties. High level fire concealment frameworks, crisis clearing systems, and cutting edge wellbeing highlights add to establishing a protected climate for the two travelers and team.

Natural contemplations are progressively incorporated into plan standards, mirroring a developing consciousness of the environmental effect of sea exercises. The investigation of green innovations, for example, wind-help frameworks like sails and rotor sails, intends to bridle sustainable power sources and diminish dependence on customary drive strategies. The utilization of cutting edge coatings and hostile to fouling materials adds to limiting the natural effect of monster ships on marine environments.

As titanic boats proceed with their excursion through the oceans, the investigation of their designing wonders broadens further into the multifaceted subtleties of their insides, framework, and the continuous endeavors to upgrade their ecological supportability.

The inside plan of giant boats is a diverse undertaking that goes past simple feel. For vessels obliging enormous quantities of travelers, for example, luxury ships, the design and conveniences assume an essential part in upgrading the general traveler experience. Engineers and fashioners work pair to make spaces that are outwardly engaging as well as practical and agreeable.

Luxury ships, specifically, feature a bunch of diversion choices, feasting settings, and sporting offices. The plan of public spaces, from terrific chambers to extensive theaters, is painstakingly coordinated to augment the utilization of accessible space while furnishing travelers with different and drawing in encounters. Specialty eateries, themed parlors, and wellbeing offices add to the general charm of these drifting hotels.

Lodge configuration is one more part of inside designing that spotlights on augmenting solace and proficiency. Ergonomically planned living spaces capitalize on accessible area, guaranteeing that travelers have a loosening up retreat to get back to in the wake of investigating the boat's conveniences. Current voyage transport lodges frequently highlight inventive capacity arrangements, convertible furnishings, and brilliant advancements to upgrade the visitor experience.

Productivity in space usage stretches out past traveler regions to team quarters and functional spaces. The everyday environments for the team, who guarantee the consistent activity of goliath ships, are painstakingly thought of. Team lodges are intended to enhance space while giving fundamental conveniences, adding to an agreeable and useful work space.

The incorporation of trend setting innovations into epic boats reaches out past route and drive to include savvy transport frameworks. These frameworks use Web of Things (IoT) gadgets, sensors, and availability to screen and oversee different parts of boat activities. Computerized frameworks add to energy productivity by advancing lighting, environment control, and other locally available cycles.

Foundation assumes an essential part in supporting the tasks of gigantic boats. Seaports and terminals are decisively designed to oblige the size and draft of these enormous vessels. Profound billets, high level freight dealing with hardware, and cutting edge security frameworks are indispensable parts of port foundation intended to work with the productive stacking and dumping of epic boats.

The coordination of savvy port advances further improves the proficiency of port tasks. Computerized cranes, advanced coordinated operations stages, and continuous checking frameworks add to smoothed out freight dealing with and quicker completion times. These advancements benefit the oceanic business as well as have more extensive ramifications for worldwide exchange and production network productivity.

Dry harbors, particular offices intended for the support and fix of boats, are fundamental parts of oceanic foundation. Epic boats might require intermittent dry-mooring for assessments, structure cleaning, and support errands. The designing behind dry harbors includes cutting edge innovations, for example, drifting dry harbors and synchronized ballasting frameworks, which empower boats to be lifted out of the water for assessment and fixes.

As titanic boats explore the untamed ocean, the natural effect of their tasks turns into a basic thought. The sea business is progressively centered around taking on reasonable practices and diminishing its natural impression. Counterbalance water treatment frameworks, for instance, forestall the spread of obtrusive species by treating and purging counterweight water before it is delivered into new conditions.

Squander the executives advances are vital to the natural manageability of gigantic boats. High level frameworks for sewage treatment, squander reusing, and dependable removal add to limiting the effect on marine biological systems. The turn of events and execution of worldwide guidelines, like the Global Oceanic Association's (IMO) MARPOL Extension VI, set principles for diminishing air contamination from ships by restricting sulfur content in energizes.

In the mission for greener impetus advances, goliath ships are investigating elective fills and energy sources. Melted Flammable gas (LNG), thought about a cleaner option in contrast to customary marine energizes, is progressively being embraced in the business. The improvement of hydrogen power devices and battery-electric impetus frameworks addresses a boondocks in practical sea transportation, offering the potential for zero-outflow tasks.

Wind-help advances, for example, sails and rotor sails, are getting momentum as creative answers for upgrade the eco-friendliness of epic boats. These frameworks outfit wind energy to enhance conventional impetus techniques, lessening fuel utilization and outflows. As the business embraces these advances, enormous boats become pioneers in the shift towards additional harmless to the ecosystem sea rehearses.

The investigation of huge boats stretches out past their sheer size and designing wonders to incorporate the multifaceted subtleties of their insides, framework, and continuous endeavors to upgrade natural maintainability. The cautious thought of traveler experience, the streamlining of functional spaces, and the mix of shrewd advancements feature the versatility and development inside the oceanic business.

Foundation, from seaports to dry harbors, shapes the foundation of help for enormous boats, guaranteeing their consistent activity and upkeep. The natural manageability of these maritime goliaths is a squeezing concern, driving the business to investigate and carry out greener innovations, elective powers, and mindful waste administration rehearses.

As huge boats explore the oceans, they address the zenith of sea designing as well as the advancing responsibility of the business to offset progress with natural stewardship. These vessels, with their complicated exchange of plan, innovation, and maintainability, act as guides of advancement on the far reaching material of the world's seas, forming the eventual fate of sea investigation and transportation.

1.3 Specific engineering challenges and solutions.

Investigating the domain of titanic boats divulges a horde of explicit designing difficulties that require inventive and complicated arrangements. From the full scale size of primary uprightness to the miniature degree of materials science, these difficulties highlight the intricacy of planning, building, and working vessels of such loftiness on the untamed ocean.

One of the chief difficulties in giant boat designing lies in the primary uprightness of these huge vessels. The sheer size and weight of enormous boats request a degree of vigor that can endure the constant powers of the vast sea. The frame, specifically, faces monstrous pressure from waves, flows, and dynamic burdens during route. Guaranteeing the primary uprightness includes fastidious plan contemplations, material choice, and development procedures.

The selection of materials is a basic consider tending to underlying difficulties. Customary wooden shipbuilding has given way to the utilization of metals, basically steel, because of its remarkable strength and sturdiness. The test lies in tracking down the right harmony among strength and weight. High-strength combinations have become fundamental to the development of huge boat frames, taking into consideration improved primary trustworthiness without settling for less on weight.

The welding of huge boat frames presents one more arrangement of difficulties. The welding system should stick to rigid quality guidelines to guarantee the dependability of the primary associations. Mechanized welding frameworks and automated advancements are progressively utilized to accomplish exact and steady welds.

These innovations not just improve the productivity of the welding system yet additionally add to the general quality and wellbeing of the vessel.

Hostile to consumption measures address a urgent answer for address the test of shielding gigantic boat structures from the destructive impacts of seawater. Defensive coatings, conciliatory anodes, and cathodic security frameworks make a hindrance against consumption, expanding the life expectancy of the vessel. The continuous innovative work of erosion safe materials and coatings add to the steady development of arrangements in this space.

Impetus frameworks for titanic boats present a multi-layered designing test, adjusting the requirement for power, proficiency, and natural maintainability. Customary impetus frameworks, like diesel motors, have been a pillar, yet the business faces expanding strain to decrease discharges and investigate elective energizes. This challenge has prodded developments in impetus advancements, prompting the reception of cleaner and more proficient choices.

Atomic drive, while progressive as far as power and perseverance, brings its own arrangement of difficulties, including security concerns and the removal of atomic waste. The reconciliation of atomic power into epic boats requires modern designing answers for address these difficulties and guarantee the protected and manageable activity of such vessels.

The mission for energy proficiency has driven the advancement of crossover impetus frameworks, joining customary motors with elective power sources like electric impetus or wind-help innovations. These crossover arrangements present a mind boggling designing test regarding incorporating different impetus frameworks, streamlining their coordination, and overseeing energy circulation ready.

Wind-help advancements, for example, sails and rotor sails, present explicit designing difficulties connected with their reconciliation into giant boats. Planning these frameworks to endure the powerful powers of wind while guaranteeing similarity with existing drive frameworks requires a fragile equilibrium. The designing arrangements include streamlined displaying, material science, and control frameworks to successfully saddle wind energy.

The inside plan of epic boats acquaints difficulties related with ergonomics, space use, and traveler experience. Making agreeable and useful living spaces inside the bounds of a monster transport includes clever arrangements in engineering plan, particular furnishings, and savvy advancements. The improvement of lodge designs, shared regions, and sporting spaces requests a fastidious way to deal with upgrade the general personal satisfaction for travelers and group.

Savvy transport frameworks, fueled by the Web of Things (IoT) and network, bring their own arrangement of designing difficulties.

Guaranteeing the unwavering quality and network safety of these interconnected frameworks requires vigorous answers for forestall expected weaknesses and digital dangers. The combination of mechanization and man-made brainpower acquaints difficulties related with framework coordination, constant information handling, and the consistent association of different boat frameworks.

Foundation challenges emerge in the development and support of gigantic boats. Dry docks, fundamental for investigations and fixes, request complex designing answers for oblige the size and weight of these vessels. The synchronization of ballasting frameworks and the utilization of drifting dry harbors address imaginative answers for lift epic boats out of the water for upkeep without expecting them to be moved to a proper dry harbor office.

Seaports and terminals intended to deal with goliath ships require specific foundation to help their activities. Profound compartments, high level freight dealing with hardware, and shrewd port innovations are designing arrangements that upgrade the proficiency of stacking and dumping tasks. The reconciliation of robotized cranes, advanced strategies stages, and ongoing observing frameworks upgrades port activities and adds to the general proficiency of oceanic exchange.

The ecological effect of epic boats requires designated designing answers for address issues, for example, counterbalance water treatment and discharges decrease. Stabilizer water treatment frameworks utilize cutting edge innovations, including filtration and bright sanitization, to forestall the spread of intrusive species. The improvement of elective fills, like Melted Flammable gas (LNG), and the investigation of hydrogen power modules address designing arrangements pointed toward decreasing the ecological impression of monster ships.

The incorporation of wind-help advances, while offering natural advantages, acquaints designing difficulties related with streamlined features, materials science, and control frameworks. Planning sails or rotor cruises that can endure the powers of wind, conform to evolving conditions, and consistently incorporate with existing drive frameworks requires a multidisciplinary approach. The continuous innovative work in this field add to refining the designing answers for viable breeze help advances.

Proceeding with the investigation of huge boats, extra designing difficulties and arrangements arise across different areas, further exhibiting the multifaceted idea of sea designing. These difficulties envelop viewpoints like security, route, and the non-stop quest for innovative progressions that reclassify the capacities of these enormous vessels.

Security contemplations address a principal designing test in the plan and activity of monster ships. The sheer size and intricacy of these vessels require hearty wellbeing elements to safeguard the two travelers and group.

High level fire concealment frameworks, crisis departure methodology, and cutting edge wellbeing innovations are coordinated into the designing plan to guarantee a solid climate ready.

Overt repetitiveness in basic frameworks is a key designing answer for improve the security of epic boats. The consolidation of reinforcement frameworks and safeguard components mitigates the gamble of framework disappointments during activity. Overt repetitiveness reaches out to imperative parts like route gear, impetus frameworks, and correspondence frameworks, guaranteeing that the boat can keep on working securely even in case of unanticipated difficulties.

Route in the huge span of the untamed ocean presents extraordinary difficulties for monster ships. High level route and control frameworks, fueled by satellite innovation and complex sensors, address these difficulties by giving exact situating and continuous data. Worldwide Situating Framework (GPS) innovation, spinners, and radar frameworks add to exact route, permitting huge boats to navigate complicated courses with certainty.

The combination of computerization into route frameworks addresses a huge designing arrangement. Incorporated span frameworks, joining different route apparatuses, improve situational mindfulness for the team. Mechanized impact evasion frameworks use sensor information to recognize likely dangers and give ideal cautions or course changes. These advancements work on the security of route as well as add to the functional productivity of epic boats.

Ecological maintainability is a general worry in current oceanic designing, and gigantic boats are no exemption. The test lies in creating and carrying out designing arrangements that limit the ecological effect of these huge vessels on marine environments and the climate. Tough guidelines, like the Worldwide Sea Association's (IMO) MARPOL Extension VI, set norms for diminishing air contamination from ships by restricting sulfur content in fills.

One of the imaginative designing answers for diminish outflows is the investigation of elective powers. Melted Petroleum gas (LNG) has acquired conspicuousness as a cleaner option in contrast to customary marine powers, offering lower outflows and further developed air quality. The reception of LNG impetus frameworks in epic boats lines up with the business' obligation to harmless to the ecosystem rehearses.

Hydrodynamics, the investigation of how water communicates with the frame of a boat, presents continuous difficulties in enhancing the presentation of huge boats. Planning frame shapes that limit opposition, upgrade steadiness, and further develop eco-friendliness requires a nuanced comprehension of liquid elements. Computational Liquid Elements (CFD) reproductions assume a significant part in tweaking structure plans, permitting designers to dissect and streamline the hydrodynamic exhibition of monster ships.

Chasing energy proficiency, wind-help innovations arise as an interesting designing arrangement. The test lies in planning and executing sails or rotor cruises that successfully saddle wind energy to enhance customary impetus techniques. The powerful idea of wind conditions, alongside the requirement for consistent reconciliation with existing drive frameworks, requests complex designing arrangements in streamlined features, materials science, and control frameworks.

The improvement of independent or semi-independent route frameworks addresses a wilderness in sea designing for goliath ships. The combination of man-made brainpower, AI, and high level sensor innovations empowers these vessels to work with diminished human mediation. Independent boats hold the commitment of expanded proficiency, lower functional expenses, and improved wellbeing. Nonetheless, the designing difficulties incorporate tending to administrative structures, guaranteeing online protection, and laying out vigorous safeguard components to ensure the protected activity of these automated vessels.

In the area of drive frameworks, the quest for manageability prompts the investigation of hydrogen power devices and battery-electric advances. Hydrogen power modules offer a perfect and productive option in contrast to customary ignition motors, transmitting just water fume as a side-effect. The test lies in creating financially savvy and versatile answers for coordinating hydrogen power devices into titanic boats, tending to stockpiling, conveyance, and security contemplations.

Battery-electric drive addresses one more road for diminishing discharges in enormous boats. Progresses in energy capacity advancements add to the improvement of high-limit batteries equipped for controlling these huge vessels. The designing test includes improving the energy thickness of batteries, overseeing charging foundation, and tending to the weight contemplations related with enormous scope battery frameworks.

Materials science keeps on being a point of convergence in tending to designing difficulties, especially in the improvement of cutting edge composites and lightweight combinations. The mission for materials with better strength-than weight proportions plans to upgrade the general load of monster ships without compromising primary honesty. Developments in materials science add to accomplishing the sensitive harmony between sturdiness, weight decrease, and natural manageability.

In the domain of framework, the test lies in adjusting ports and terminals to oblige the developing requirements of huge boats. The rising size of these vessels requires profound compartments, extended freight taking care of abilities, and shrewd port advancements. The designing arrangements include the plan and development of port offices that can proficiently deal with the stacking and dumping of epiç boats, adding to the general effectiveness of sea operations.

Dry harbors, fundamental for the support and fix of enormous boats, face moves in adjusting to the particular prerequisites of these monstrous vessels. The designing arrangements incorporate the plan of bigger and more strong dry docks furnished with cutting edge lifting and ballasting frameworks. These offices are fundamental for assessing, fixing, and keeping up with goliath ships, guaranteeing their proceeded with security.

The particular designing difficulties and arrangements in the domain of huge boats length a wide range, enveloping wellbeing, route, ecological maintainability, impetus frameworks, materials science, and foundation. The tireless quest for advancement and the use of multidisciplinary designing arrangements portray the development of oceanic designing. Gigantic boats, with their unpredictable plan and trend setting innovations, epitomize the finish of human creativity as they explore the world's seas, defying and defeating the perplexing difficulties presented by the powerful oceanic climate.

Chapter 2

Giants on the Horizon

"Monsters Not too far off" typifies the remarkable adventure of enormous boats, their development, designing wonders, and the significant effect they have on the sea scene. As these sea behemoths navigate the immense breadths of the world's seas, their importance reaches out past simple vessels, exemplifying a union of human inventiveness, innovative headway, and the determined quest for progress.

At the core of this story is the development of goliath ships — an excursion that traverses hundreds of years and exemplifies the quintessence of sea investigation and exchange. From the simple vessels that considered exploring unfamiliar waters to the cutting edge leviathans that beauty the oceans today, the development of gigantic boats is a demonstration of human assurance and the interminable journey for revelation.

The starting points of enormous boats can be followed back to the early civilizations that depended on oceanic exchange for food and thriving. Old nautical societies, like the Phoenicians, Egyptians, and Greeks, established the groundworks for shipbuilding methods and navigational ability. Their vessels, however unassuming in contrast with contemporary monster ships, addressed the primary sections in the unfurling epic of oceanic investigation.

The Period of Investigation in the fifteenth and sixteenth hundreds of years introduced another time for huge boats. As European powers looked for new shipping lanes and regions, they wandered into unfamiliar waters with vessels like caravels and ships. These wooden goliaths, moved by the two sails and paddles, set out on trying journeys that extended the explored parts of the planet and reclassified the extent of oceanic prospects.

The coming of the Modern Upheaval in the eighteenth and nineteenth hundreds of years denoted a significant second in the development of enormous boats. The progress from sail to steam power reformed oceanic transportation. Iron and steel frames supplanted wooden designs, offering uncommon strength and toughness.

Steam motors, controlled by coal and later oil, pushed goliath ships with recently discovered speed and dependability, changing worldwide exchange and availability.

The twentieth century saw the ascent of maritime monsters and traveler liners that pushed the limits of sea designing. Ships like the Iowa-class and Yamato-class represented maritime power, extending force across immense seas. At the same time, lavish sea liners, for example, the RMS Titanic and Sovereign Mary encapsulated extravagance and tastefulness, taking care of the expanding period of transoceanic travel.

The post-The Second Great War time frame saw the rise of containerization, a progressive idea that changed the coordinated operations and financial matters of oceanic exchange. Holder ships, with their normalized freight units, smoothed out stacking and dumping processes, making ready for the advanced time of enormous boats. The sheer size of these vessels, equipped for conveying huge number of holders, reclassified the productivity and size of worldwide transportation.

The contemporary scene of epic boats is overwhelmed by compartment vessels, mass transporters, oil big haulers, and luxury ships that push the limits of size and limit. The designing accomplishments expected to build and work these oceanic goliaths are completely phenomenal. The cutting edge oceanic industry mirrors a combination of state of the art innovations, manageable practices, and the getting through mission for productivity.

The designing wonders of monster ships are appeared in the perplexing subtleties of their plan and development. Maritime design, a discipline that joins workmanship and science, assumes a significant part in molding these vessels for ideal execution. PC supported plan (computer aided design) and reenactment innovations permit maritime draftsmen to demonstrate and refine each part of a boat's construction, from its hydrodynamics to its inward format.

The development cycle itself is an ensemble of accuracy and scale. Gigantic ships frequently go through measured development, with various areas manufactured freely and gathered later.

This secluded methodology speeds up the development course of events as well as takes into consideration the concurrent work on numerous areas. Shipbuilders convey progressed welding procedures, including automated welding, to guarantee the respectability of the structure, the foundation of any enormous boat.

Materials science remains at the very front of designing enormous boats. The shift from wood to metals like steel and aluminum has been instrumental in improving the underlying uprightness of these vessels. High-strength amalgams further brace transport bodies, permitting them to endure the cruel states of the untamed ocean. The continuous investigation of cutting edge composites and lightweight materials keeps on reclassifying the conceivable outcomes of boat development, offsetting strength with weight proficiency.

The drive frameworks of gigantic boats address a mechanical boondocks where development meets ecological maintainability. While customary boats depended on sails or steam motors, current vessels frequently highlight diesel-electric, gas turbine, or even atomic drive. The decision of impetus relies upon the planned utilization of the boat, be it business transportation, maritime activities, or logical exploration.

In the domain of energy proficiency, enormous boats are pioneers in taking on green advancements. Slow-steaming, an act of working boats at lower velocities to streamline fuel utilization, has turned into a typical technique to decrease emanations. The investigation of elective fills like melted petroleum gas (LNG), biofuels, and hydrogen mirrors the business' obligation to relieving its ecological effect.

Route and control frameworks have gone through a groundbreaking development, consolidating trend setting innovations to guarantee the wellbeing and mobility of goliath ships. Worldwide Situating Framework (GPS) innovation, radar frameworks, and robotized route helps empower exact course plotting and impact evasion. The reconciliation of man-made reasoning and mechanization further upgrades the functional proficiency of these oceanic goliaths.

The insides of goliath ships, particularly luxury ships, address a combination of designing and neighborliness. The test lies in planning spaces that oblige huge number of travelers for expanded periods while giving solace, diversion, and wellbeing. Ergonomics, measured plan, and the mix of brilliant innovations add to making living and sporting spaces that rival those ashore.

Foundation custom-made for gigantic boats stretches out past the actual vessels. Seaports and terminals are designed to deal with the sheer size and draft of these sea behemoths. Profound compartments, high level freight taking care of hardware, and best in class security frameworks describe current port offices. The combination of shrewd port advancements, including computerized cranes and advanced planned operations stages, smoothes out the progression of merchandise and upgrades the proficiency of oceanic exchange.

Dry harbors, fundamental for the upkeep and fix of giant boats, grandstand their own designing ability. These offices, frequently furnished with drifting dry harbors and synchronized ballasting frameworks, empower boats to go through assessments, structure cleaning, and support assignments without being removed from the water. Remotely worked submerged vehicles (ROVs) and high level welding procedures further add to limiting free time during upkeep tasks.

The natural effect of monster ships has turned into a point of convergence in sea designing. Counterbalance water treatment frameworks forestall the spread of intrusive species by sanitizing weight water before release. Discharge control advances, like scrubbers and specific reactant decrease (SCR) frameworks, diminish the poisons delivered high up. The investigation of wind-help innovations, for example, sails and rotor sails, adds a practical aspect to impetus frameworks.

Security contemplations saturate each part of designing titanic boats. Progressed firefighting frameworks, crisis departure techniques, and extensive wellbeing highlights guarantee that these vessels can endure unexpected difficulties. The fuse of overt repetitiveness in basic frameworks, alongside consistent headways in wellbeing advances, mirrors a promise to shielding the existences of travelers and group.

The skyline of monster ships reaches out past the ordinary domain with the investigation of independent and remotely worked vessels. Automated surface vessels (USVs) and independent submerged vehicles (AUVs) address the bleeding edge of oceanic innovation. The designing difficulties in this area rotate around creating solid independent frameworks, tending to administrative structures, and guaranteeing the network safety of automated vessels.

As enormous boats keep on exploring the world's seas, their outline not too far off represents something beyond oceanic transportation. They are drifting urban communities, worldwide connectors, and demonstrations of human inventiveness. The difficulties looked in designing these sea goliaths reflect the difficulties of our interconnected world — the mission for supportability, the harmony among progress and natural obligation, and the persistent quest for development.

The adventure of gigantic boats unfurls as an embroidery woven with strings of development, difficulties, and arrangements, exhibiting the strength of human designing notwithstanding the tremendous and capricious seas. Digging further into this story uncovers the mind boggling dance of innovation, manageability, and cultural necessities that shape the present and fate of these sea goliaths.

Innovation, a main impetus behind the development of giant boats, has introduced a time of extraordinary network and proficiency. The combination of Web of Things (IoT) gadgets and brilliant advances improves the functional capacities of these vessels.

Condition-based checking frameworks, prescient upkeep, and continuous information examination add to the proactive administration of monster ships, limiting free time and enhancing execution.

Satellite correspondence frameworks further associate goliath boats to worldwide organizations, guaranteeing consistent correspondence no matter what their area on the vast ocean. This availability works with route and functional effectiveness as well as supports the prosperity of travelers and group by empowering consistent correspondence and admittance to fundamental administrations.

The drive frameworks of epic boats address a wilderness where ecological manageability combines with mechanical development. The investigation of elective energizes, for example, biofuels got from sustainable sources, lines up with the business' obligation to lessening its carbon impression. The improvement of half breed drive frameworks, joining customary motors with electric impetus, offers an adaptable and eco-accommodating way to deal with fueling these sea behemoths.

Electric impetus frameworks, driven by progressions in battery innovation, are getting momentum as a practical other option. Battery-electric impetus diminishes emanations, commotion contamination, and the dependence on customary non-renewable energy sources. The designing difficulties in this domain include upgrading energy stockpiling limits, overseeing charging framework, and guaranteeing the security and productivity of enormous scope battery frameworks.

Hydrogen energy units address one more encouraging road for economical drive in gigantic boats. The utilization of hydrogen as a perfect energy source offers the potential for zero-outflow tasks. Designing arrangements center around the improvement of proficient energy unit frameworks, hydrogen capacity innovations, and the foundation of a hydrogen inventory network for sea applications.

The undeniable trends blow through the sails of goliath ships, straightforwardly, as wind-help advances experience a resurgence in interest. Sails and rotor sails saddle the force of the breeze to enhance customary drive techniques, diminishing fuel utilization and outflows. The designing difficulties in carrying out wind-help advancements include planning sails that can endure differing wind conditions, enhancing their reconciliation with existing drive frameworks, and guaranteeing functional productivity across different sea conditions.

Materials science keeps on being a main thrust in the mission for lighter, more grounded, and more reasonable materials for goliath ships. High level composites, built up plastics, and nanomaterials are being investigated to lessen the heaviness of boat structures without compromising strength. The utilization of bio-based materials and recyclable composites lines up with the business' obligation to harmless to the ecosystem rehearses.

The insides of gigantic boats, especially luxury ships, are a material for the marriage of designing and extravagance. Inside plan developments center around expanding space use, upgrading traveler solace, and incorporating savvy innovations for a consistent encounter. The test lies in offsetting feel with usefulness, establishing vivid conditions that take care of the assorted requirements and inclinations of travelers.

The cultural effect of huge boats stretches out past the prompt domains of transportation and exchange. Luxury ships, specifically, are drifting microcosms of amusement, recreation, and social trade. The designing test in planning these vessels includes making spaces that take special care of different socioeconomics, giving a range of encounters going from connoisseur eating and Broadway-style shows to health offices and vivid amusement parks.

Openness and inclusivity are key contemplations in the designing of enormous boats' insides. The plan of public spaces, lodges, and conveniences should oblige travelers with shifting portability needs, guaranteeing that the voyage experience is open to all. Lifts, inclines, and other assistive innovations add to a more comprehensive and inviting climate ready.

The worldwide effect of huge boats resounds in the financial corridors of global exchange. The productive transportation of merchandise by means of holder ships is a key part of the worldwide inventory network. Enormous holder vessels, with their transcending piles of normalized freight compartments, typify the scale and productivity of current sea exchange. The designing difficulties in this area include upgrading holder stowage, guaranteeing soundness during stacking and dumping, and boosting freight limit.

Ports and terminals, as the nexus among land and ocean, assume a significant part in supporting the tasks of gigantic boats. The designing of port offices includes adjusting to the developing necessities of these vessels, from obliging bigger drafts to carrying out cutting edge freight dealing with advancements. Robotized cranes, advanced planned operations stages, and constant observing frameworks add to the proficiency and throughput of present day ports.

Dry harbors, the safe-havens for giant boats during upkeep and fixes, are advancing to fulfill the needs of bigger and more complicated vessels. Drifting dry docks, synchronized ballasting frameworks, and submerged review innovations empower effective and exhaustive upkeep without the need to dock the vessel in a decent dry dock. The designing arrangements in this domain plan to limit free time, decrease ecological effect, and guarantee the life span of sea resources.

As gigantic boats keep on exploring the seas, they stand up to the basic of ecological obligation. The effect of transportation on marine environments, including issues, for example, weight water release and submerged commotion contamination, is a point of convergence of sea designing. Maintainable practices, for example, balance water treatment frameworks and the utilization of eco-accommodating structure coatings, add to limiting the biological impression of titanic boats.

In the domain of security, designing arrangements go past the customary proportions of firefighting frameworks and departure techniques. The coordination of man-made reasoning, AI, and sensor advances empowers prescient wellbeing investigation. These frameworks examine information from different installed sensors to distinguish potential wellbeing perils, considering proactive gamble the executives and preventive measures.

The continuous investigation of independent and remotely worked vessels addresses a change in outlook in sea designing. Automated surface vessels (USVs) and independent submerged vehicles (AUVs) are at the bleeding edge of this mechanical outskirts. The designing difficulties include creating dependable independent frameworks, tending to administrative structures, and guaranteeing the network safety of automated vessels.

"Monsters Not too far off" encapsulate more than the actual presence of gigantic boats on the untamed ocean. They address a combination of innovation, maintainability, and cultural goals. The story of these oceanic goliaths is one of steady development, driven by the collaboration of designing development, natural stewardship, and the steadily changing requirements of an associated world. As titanic boats explore the skyline, they convey freight and travelers as well as the yearnings of an industry focused on pushing the limits of what is possible on the amazing phase of the world's seas.

2.1 A journey through the timeline of significant maritime advancements.

Setting out on an ordered excursion through the chronicles of sea history uncovers an embroidery woven with development, investigation, and the dauntless human soul. From the simple vessels that thought for even a second to explore unknown waters to the state of the art innovations driving current oceanic goliaths, this story follows the development of critical sea progressions that have molded the course of human civilization.

The earliest sections of oceanic history unfurl with the development of nautical societies in times long past. The Phoenicians, prestigious as talented guides, set forth across the Mediterranean, laying out shipping lanes and sea networks that established the groundwork for early oceanic trade. The Egyptians, as well, explored the Nile and wandered into the Red Ocean, exhibiting early accomplishments of route and shipbuilding.

The Greeks, in the seventh century BCE, presented the warship, a kitchen moved by three banks of paddles, reforming maritime fighting and exchange. This period denoted the convergence of oceanic ability and key impact, as the Greek city-states extended their sea areas and took part in nautical campaigns that arrived at the most distant corners of the well explored regions of the planet.

The Roman Domain, acquiring oceanic information from its ancestors, further high level maritime designing with the presentation of the corvus, a loading up gadget that improved their strength adrift. The Roman naval force turned into an impressive power in the Mediterranean, protecting shipping lanes and getting the realm's sea borders.

As the old world blurred into the middle age time, oceanic investigation saw a resurgence during the Period of Revelation in the fifteenth hundred years. The caravel, a flexible and flexibility transport, arose as the vessel of decision for voyagers like Christopher Columbus and Vasco da Gama. These courageous mariners thought for even a moment to wander into unfamiliar waters, circumnavigating the globe and laying out oceanic associations that reshaped the well explored regions of the planet.

The seventeenth century introduced the time of tall boats, portrayed by their transcending poles and various sails. The boat of-the-line, furnished with strong guns, turned into the foundation of maritime armadas during the Period of Sail. The oceanic scene was overwhelmed by maritime powers like Britain, France, and Spain, taking part in maritime fighting and worldwide investigation.

The nineteenth century saw a change in outlook in sea impetus with the coming of steam power. The steamship, typified by vessels like the SS Extraordinary England, reformed sea transportation by offering dependable and effective drive. The change from sail to steam denoted a groundbreaking time, as steam motors empowered boats to explore contrary to the natural flow and cross longer distances with more prominent speed.

The mid-nineteenth century saw the introduction of the ironclad warship, an imposing vessel safeguarded by iron defensive layer. The USS Screen and the CSS Virginia, heroes in the Skirmish of Hampton Streets during the American Nationwide conflict, proclaimed another period in maritime fighting. The improvement of ironclads prepared for the possible predominance of steel-hulled ships, denoting a urgent second in sea designing.

The late nineteenth and mid twentieth hundreds of years saw the pinnacle of extravagance sea liners, exemplified by the RMS Titanic and the RMS Sovereign Mary. These vessels, enhanced with lavish insides and taking care of overseas travel, addressed the exemplification of sea polish. The awfulness of the Titanic, sinking on its first trip in 1912, highlighted the requirement for upgraded security estimates in oceanic designing.

The two Universal Conflicts of the twentieth century moved sea innovation higher than ever. Submarines, at first presented in the nineteenth hundred years, assumed an essential part in maritime procedures during the two contentions. The improvement of plane carrying warships, exemplified by the USS Undertaking, denoted a progressive change in maritime power projection. The combination of avionics with sea activities re-imagined the extent of maritime fighting.

Post-The Second Great War, the shipper marine went through an extreme change with the coming of containerization. The compartment transport, spearheaded by Malcom McLean during the 1950s, normalized freight taking care of and changed worldwide exchange. The containerization unrest smoothed out stacking and dumping processes, decreasing times required to circle back in ports and altogether bringing down transportation costs.

The last 50% of the twentieth century saw the ascent of atomic controlled submarines and surface vessels. The USS Nautilus, charged in 1954, turned into the world's most memorable functional atomic fueled submarine, exhibiting the potential for expanded submerged activities. Atomic drive offered unmatched perseverance and vital capacities, setting its place in maritime arms stockpiles.

The late twentieth 100 years and mid 21st century saw a mechanical renaissance in oceanic designing. The coming of satellite route, with the Worldwide Situating Framework (GPS) specifically, changed sea route by giving exact situating information to vessels anyplace on The planet. GPS innovation turned into a fundamental apparatus for route, security, and search and salvage activities.

The investigation of the remote ocean entered another time with the advancement of subs and remotely worked vehicles (ROVs). The Trieste, in 1960, dropped to the Challenger Profound, the most profound point in the sea, denoting a memorable accomplishment in remote ocean investigation. The ensuing improvement of ROVs considered maintained and controlled investigation of the sea floor, revealing secrets in the profundities.

In the domain of oceanic wellbeing, the Worldwide Sea Association (IMO) arose as a central member in laying out worldwide guidelines and guidelines. The Global Show for the Wellbeing of Life Adrift (SOLAS), started in 1914, went through numerous modifications, with the SOLAS 1974 show turning into a milestone system for oceanic security guidelines. The execution of SOLAS norms has altogether added to upgrading the wellbeing of vessels and protecting lives adrift.

The turn of the thousand years delivered a flood of development in sea innovation. Automated surface vessels (USVs) and independent submerged vehicles (AUVs) arose as state of the art stages for oceanic activities. USVs, moved by cutting edge sensor advances and man-made brainpower, exhibited their true capacity in errands like observation, surveillance, and ecological checking. AUVs, then again, showed their ability for independent investigation and information assortment in the remote ocean.

The investigation of sustainable power sources stretched out to sea applications with the improvement of wind-help advances. Sails, rotor sails, and kite impetus frameworks arose as practical answers for outfit wind energy and increase customary drive strategies.

These innovations, while harkening back to the period of sail, integrate current materials and designing to upgrade effectiveness and lessen fuel utilization.

The 21st century likewise saw the investigation of elective fills for oceanic impetus. Condensed Petroleum gas (LNG), with its lower discharges profile contrasted with conventional marine energizes, acquired noticeable quality as a cleaner choice for fueling ships. The business' quest for maintainability prompted explores different avenues regarding biofuels, hydrogen power modules, and battery-electric drive, mirroring a guarantee to diminishing the ecological effect of oceanic tasks.

Oceanic network arrived at new levels with the appearance of satellite correspondence and broadband innovations. High-throughput satellite frameworks worked with constant correspondence, web access, and information move on board vessels. This network upgraded navigational abilities as well as worked on the personal satisfaction for sailors by empowering admittance to correspondence, diversion, and instructive assets.

The designing of giant boats, portrayed by compartment vessels, mass transporters, oil big haulers, and luxury ships, developed because of the requests of worldwide exchange and transportation. The scale and intricacy of these vessels required headways in maritime design, materials science, drive frameworks, and security highlights. Titanic boats became images of human accomplishment, interfacing mainlands and working with the development of merchandise and individuals on an exceptional scale.

The continuous investigation of the Cold locale for sea courses and assets addresses a boondocks in contemporary oceanic progressions. The subsiding ice covers and the launch of the Northern Ocean Course have started interest in the advancement of ice-class vessels and particular innovations for polar route. The Icy's essential significance in worldwide delivery courses and asset extraction highlights the developing difficulties and open doors in oceanic designing.

As we explore the flows of the present, the skyline of oceanic headways keeps on growing. The combination of man-made consciousness, AI, and huge information examination holds the commitment of further improving the productivity, wellbeing, and maintainability of oceanic tasks. Brilliant delivery, described by the Web of Things (IoT) applications and independent frameworks, proclaims another time of availability and computerization in the oceanic business.

In the contemporary scene of sea headways, supportability has arisen as a characterizing rule, guiding the course of development and designing. The oceanic business, insightful of its natural impression, has embraced a change in outlook toward eco-accommodating practices and innovations.

This shift is especially clear in the investigation of elective energizes and drive frameworks that decrease discharges and moderate the business' effect on environmental change.

The basic for manageability in oceanic impetus is highlighted by the Worldwide Sea Association's (IMO) severe guidelines pointed toward checking ozone depleting substance outflows from ships. Thus, the business has seen a flood in the reception of elective powers, with melted gaseous petrol (LNG) at the front line. LNG, a cleaner-consuming fuel with lower sulfur content, has acquired conspicuousness for its capability to diminish carbon dioxide emanations as well as different poisons related with conventional marine fills.

Hydrogen power modules address one more boondocks in manageable oceanic impetus. Hydrogen, when utilized as a fuel, radiates just water fume as a side-effect, offering a zero-discharge option in contrast to regular fills. The designing difficulties in executing hydrogen power modules on ships include creating proficient capacity and conveyance frameworks, guaranteeing security, and tending to the monetary reasonability of this imaginative innovation. Pilot tasks and exploration drives are in progress to investigate the attainability of hydrogen-controlled vessels in certifiable sea activities.

Battery-electric drive has arisen as a suitable and promising answer for lessening outflows in sea transport. Propels in energy capacity advances have prompted the improvement of high-limit batteries fit for fueling huge vessels. The coordination of battery-electric frameworks in half breed setups, joined with conventional motors, gives an adaptable and eco-accommodating way to deal with sea impetus. Nonetheless, the designing difficulties incorporate upgrading the energy thickness of batteries, overseeing charging foundation, and tending to the weight contemplations related with huge scope battery frameworks.

Wind-help advancements, roused by the deep rooted practice of bridling wind power for drive, have encountered a resurgence in the mission for economical oceanic arrangements. Sails, rotor sails, and kite drive frameworks are being investigated as means to enhance conventional motors and diminish fuel utilization. These innovations influence the force of the breeze to drive vessels, offering an inexhaustible and outflows free wellspring of energy. The test lies in advancing the combination of wind-help advancements with existing impetus frameworks and adjusting them to different oceanic conditions.

The investigation of biofuels, got from inexhaustible sources like green growth or byproducts, lines up with the oceanic business' obligation to feasible practices. Biofuels offer the possibility to essentially diminish fossil fuel byproducts and add to a roundabout economy by using natural materials that would somehow go to squander. Notwithstanding, the versatility and cost-viability of biofuels stay key contemplations in their boundless reception as a standard oceanic fuel.

The idea of round economy standards stretches out past biofuels to the reusing and reusing of materials in transport development and support. Economical shipbreaking rehearses intend to limit natural effect by reusing steel and different materials from decommissioned vessels. The mindful removal of boat parts and adherence to natural guidelines add to lessening the environmental impression of oceanic exercises.

In the domain of oceanic security, mechanical progressions keep on forming the scene. Automated surface vessels (USVs) and independent submerged vehicles (AUVs) are at the front of advancement in sea observation, surveillance, and ecological checking. These independent frameworks, outfitted with cutting edge sensors and computerized reasoning, improve situational mindfulness and add to additional powerful oceanic tasks. Nonetheless, the combination of independent advances likewise delivers difficulties connected with administrative systems, online protection, and the moral contemplations of automated activities.

The designing spotlight on wellbeing reaches out to the improvement of canny route frameworks, crash aversion innovations, and prescient examination. The reconciliation of man-made consciousness and AI calculations empowers vessels to settle on continuous choices in light of ecological circumstances, traffic examples, and possible dangers. This proactive way to deal with security addresses a critical jump forward in the mission for mishap counteraction and chance moderation in oceanic tasks.

As the sea business keeps on exploring the intricacies of the 21st 100 years, the skyline of headways stretches out to digitalization and network. Shrewd transportation, described by the Web of Things (IoT), information investigation, and continuous observing, changes vessels into associated stages fit for advancing execution, decreasing margin time, and improving functional effectiveness. The digitalization of oceanic activities additionally adds to more proficient course arranging, fuel utilization enhancement, and smoothed out planned operations.

The continuous excursion through the timetable of oceanic progressions uncovers a story that entwines custom with development, need with supportability. From antiquated nautical societies to the state of the art advances of the 21st hundred years, the sea business has ceaselessly adjusted to the difficulties and open doors introduced by the world's seas. The ongoing accentuation on supportability, elective fills, and digitalization mirrors a guarantee to exploring the future with natural stewardship, effectiveness, and wellbeing at the front. As the sea scene keeps on developing, the narrative of sea designing unfurls as a demonstration of human creativity and flexibility notwithstanding the immense and dynamic seas.

2.2 Exploration of how the demand for larger and more specialized vessels evolved over time.

The interest for bigger and more particular vessels has gone through an extraordinary development, molded by an intersection of elements crossing monetary, innovative, and vital contemplations.

This investigation dives into the authentic setting, financial drivers, and mechanical headways that have moved the oceanic business toward the development of epic boats with explicit functionalities.

In the early ages of sea exchange, the interest for bigger vessels arose naturally as civilizations looked to grow their monetary arrive at through abroad business. The Phoenicians, Egyptians, and Greeks, trailblazers of old nautical, created bigger boats to oblige developing volumes of exchange products. The development of vessels with expanded freight limit became basic for the prospering sea economies of these antiquated civic establishments, starting the trend for the interest for bigger vessels driven by financial inspirations.

The Period of Investigation in the fifteenth and sixteenth hundreds of years denoted a vital crossroads in the interest for bigger vessels. European powers, prodded by a journey for new shipping lanes and regions, tried to configuration ships able to do long overseas journeys. The caravel, a flexible and secure vessel, exemplified the interest for specific ships that could explore both vast oceans and shallow beach front waters. The bigger size and improved navigational capacities of these vessels were fundamental for undertaking aggressive excursions and laying out worldwide exchange organizations.

The development of maritime power likewise assumed a urgent part in the interest for bigger and all the more remarkable warships. The boat of-the-line, portrayed by different weapon decks and impressive capability, turned into the highlight of maritime armadas during the Time of Sail. The interest for these enormous warships was driven by the essential basic to extend power across immense sea spaces. The sheer scale and capability of these vessels highlighted the essential significance of maritime predominance in getting shipping lanes and attesting international impact.

The Modern Unrest in the eighteenth and nineteenth hundreds of years denoted a mechanical watershed that further impacted the interest for bigger vessels. The change from sail to steam power altered sea transportation. The interest for bigger freight vessels outfitted with steam motors was powered by the requirement for quicker and more dependable vehicle of merchandise. The designing headways of the Modern Upheaval, remembering the utilization of iron and later steel for transport development, worked with the improvement of bigger and more hearty vessels.

The interest for particular vessels took a jump forward with the rise of traveler liners in the late nineteenth and mid twentieth hundreds of years. The RMS Titanic, sent off in 1912, encapsulated the interest for extravagant and mechanically progressed sea liners. These vessels were planned for proficient overseas travel as well as to offer a sumptuous encounter for travelers.

The interest for particular insides, locally available conveniences, and security highlights drove the advancement of traveler liners into drifting castles, setting new guidelines for oceanic extravagance and solace.

The Second Great War and The Second Great War introduced another time of maritime interest, described by the requirement for bigger and all the more mechanically progressed warships. Warships like the Iowa-class and plane carrying warships, for example, the USS Venture became notorious images of maritime power. The interest for these titanic warships was powered by the essential basic to extend force across tremendous seas and participate in maritime fighting on a worldwide scale.

The specific plan and weaponry of these vessels mirrored the developing idea of oceanic clash.

The post-The Second Great War time frame saw a change in perspective in the interest for particular vessels with the coming of containerization. The holder transport, a progressive idea presented by Malcom McLean during the 1950s, changed the sea business. The interest for bigger holder vessels was driven by the requirement for effective and normalized freight transport. These vessels, portrayed by their transcending piles of compartments, smoothed out the stacking and dumping processes, fundamentally diminishing completion times in ports and upsetting worldwide exchange.

Big hauler ships, intended for the vehicle of fluid freight like oil and synthetics, additionally saw an expansion popular during the mid-twentieth hundred years. The worldwide reliance on oil as an essential energy source filled the requirement for bigger and more specific big hauler vessels. The designing difficulties of building vessels able to do securely shipping gigantic amounts of unpredictable fluids prompted advancements in structure plan, wellbeing highlights, and natural assurance measures.

The interest for particular vessels kept on developing in light of the changing elements of worldwide exchange and energy utilization. The ascent of seaward oil and gas investigation in the last 50% of the twentieth century prodded the interest for particular seaward help vessels, boring apparatuses, and drifting creation stages. These vessels were intended to work in testing seaward conditions, offering calculated help and foundation for the extraction of hydrocarbons from underneath the seabed.

The interest for bigger and more refined maritime vessels persevered in the last 50% of the twentieth hundred years and into the 21st 100 years. Atomic controlled submarines and plane carrying warships became vital parts of maritime armadas, displaying headways in impetus innovation and key abilities. The interest for these particular vessels mirrored the international scene and the requirement for maritime powers equipped for expanded tasks and power projection.

The journey business, arising as a critical player in oceanic trade, has filled the interest for gigantic luxury ships. These vessels, intended for recreation travel, address an intermingling of designing greatness and friendliness development. The interest for bigger journey ships is impelled by the cutthroat idea of the business, with voyage lines competing to offer travelers steadily extending conveniences, diversion choices, and sumptuous facilities.

The contemporary interest for specific vessels stretches out to the investigation of the Icy locale. The subsiding ice covers and the kickoff of new oceanic courses have prompted the requirement for ice-class vessels fit for exploring polar waters. Icebreakers, research vessels, and freight ships intended for Cold circumstances mirror the advancing interest for vessels customized to explicit natural difficulties.

Mechanical progressions in ongoing many years have additionally powered the interest for particular vessels. The investigation of remote ocean assets has prompted the advancement of submarines and remotely worked vehicles (ROVs) intended for remote ocean investigation and mining. These vessels, outfitted with cutting edge sensors and mechanical capacities, empower the extraction of minerals and assets from the sea floor.

The interest for particular vessels in the 21st century is portrayed by an emphasis on manageability and ecological obligation. The oceanic business is seeing a flood in the interest for vessels fueled by elective powers, furnished with cutting edge outflow control innovations, and planned with energy-proficient highlights. The push for greener delivery rehearses mirrors the worldwide basic to diminish the ecological effect of sea exercises.

The investigation of seaward environmentally friendly power sources, like breeze and flowing energy, has brought about the interest for vessels fit for introducing and keeping up with seaward wind ranches and flowing energy gadgets. These specific vessels assume an essential part in the improvement of perfect and maintainable energy arrangements, adding to the continuous energy progress.

The interest for bigger and more specific vessels keeps on advancing because of the powerful powers molding the sea business in the 21st 100 years. The continuous investigation of elective powers and impetus frameworks has arisen as a characterizing factor in reshaping the interest for vessels, with an uplifted spotlight on maintainability, proficiency, and ecological obligation.

One of the unmistakable patterns affecting the interest for vessels is the investigation of elective fills to decrease the ecological effect of sea transportation. Condensed Flammable gas (LNG), as a cleaner-consuming fuel, has gotten forward momentum, especially in the domain of compartment transportation and traveler vessels. The interest for LNG-controlled vessels is driven by the craving to bring down ozone harming substance discharges and agree with progressively severe natural guidelines.

Hydrogen, proclaimed as a zero-discharge fuel while delivered utilizing environmentally friendly power sources, has likewise arisen as a point of convergence in the interest for specific vessels. Hydrogen energy components, which produce power through a synthetic response among hydrogen and oxygen, offer the potential for reasonable drive. The interest for vessels outfitted with hydrogen energy units is pushed by the business' obligation to accomplishing carbon-unbiased tasks and moderating the effect of transportation on environmental change.

Battery-electric drive addresses one more wilderness in the mission for maintainable sea arrangements. The interest for vessels fueled by huge scope battery frameworks has developed, driven by headways in energy capacity advances. Battery-electric drive lessens discharges as well as adds to calmer and all the more harmless to the ecosystem sea tasks. The interest for electric ships, beach front vessels, and short-ocean transporting arrangements highlights the business' progress toward cleaner energy options.

Wind-help advances have encountered a renaissance, offering a mix of custom and development in light of the interest for vessels with diminished fuel utilization. Sails, rotor sails, and kite impetus frameworks tackle the force of the breeze to enhance conventional drive techniques. The interest for wind-help advancements is roused by the possibility to accomplish fuel reserve funds and lessening fossil fuel byproducts, lining up with the business' quest for maintainable and savvy arrangements.

The investigation of biofuels got from inexhaustible sources has likewise affected the interest for vessels with decreased carbon impressions. Biofuels, delivered from natural materials like green growth or byproducts, offer a feasible option in contrast to regular petroleum products. The interest for vessels fit for utilizing biofuels is essential for the more extensive obligation to bio-based arrangements that add to a roundabout economy and backing the change to additional manageable sea rehearses.

The interest for vessels stretches out past the drive framework to the more extensive idea of eco-accommodating boat plan. The business is seeing an expanded spotlight on vessel enhancement, hydrodynamic proficiency, and the utilization of cutting edge materials to decrease fuel utilization and emanations. The interest for vessels planned with energy-effective highlights mirrors a comprehensive way to deal with manageabil-ity, where each part of boat configuration adds to ecological stewardship.

Notwithstanding ecological contemplations, innovative progressions are molding the interest for vessels with improved digitalization and network. The idea of savvy delivering, portrayed by the mix of Web of Things (IoT) gadgets, information exami-nation, and constant checking, is affecting the interest for vessels equipped for utilizing computerized advances for further developed productivity and wellbeing. The interest for vessels furnished with cutting edge route frameworks, prescient upkeep abilities, and independent functionalities mirrors the business' obligation to embracing the advanced change.

The interest for specific vessels likewise reaches out to the domain of seaward sustainable power. As the world changes toward cleaner and more economical energy sources, there is a developing interest for vessels intended for the establishment, support, and activity of seaward wind ranches and flowing energy projects. These par-ticular vessels assume a urgent part in supporting the extension of sustainable power framework, adding to the worldwide endeavors to moderate environmental change.

The investigation of the Icy district has introduced remarkable difficulties and amazing open doors, affecting the interest for ice-class vessels fit for exploring polar waters. As the Icy turns out to be more available because of environmental change, the interest for vessels intended to work in outrageous virus conditions is on the ascent. Icebreakers, research vessels, and freight ships prepared for Icy route are popular as sea partners position themselves to take advantage of the arising open doors in the polar district.

The interest for particular vessels isn't restricted to freight and traveler transport; it likewise includes the field of sea examination and investigation. Vessels outfitted with cutting edge sonar frameworks, subs, and remotely worked vehicles (ROVs) are pur-sued for remote ocean investigation and logical examination. The interest for research vessels equipped for leading far reaching concentrates on marine biological systems, geography, and biodiversity mirrors a guarantee to understanding and safeguarding the seas.

The sea business is likewise seeing a flood in the interest for vessels furnished with cutting edge wellbeing elements and crisis reaction capacities. Search and salvage vessels, furnished with cutting edge correspondence frameworks and life-saving advances, assume a basic part in guaranteeing the wellbeing of sailors in trouble. The interest for vessels intended to deal with crisis circumstances, including oil slicks and oceanic catastrophes, highlights the business' devotion to shielding human lives and safeguarding the marine climate.

The interest for bigger and more specific vessels is going through a groundbreaking movement, directed by the goals of maintainability, mechanical development, and advancing monetary scenes. The sea business, discerning of its part in an impacting world, is molding the interest for vessels that not just meet the momentum needs of worldwide exchange and investigation yet in addition line up with a future portrayed by natural obligation and computerized network. As the business keeps on exploring strange waters, the interest for vessels will be characterized by an amicable harmony between financial suitability, mechanical progression, and an unfaltering obligation to protecting the wellbeing and trustworthiness of our seas.

2.3 Highlighting key moments that marked a shift in the scale and capabilities of maritime giants.

The oceanic business has seen key minutes since the beginning of time that undeniable extraordinary changes in the scale and capacities of sea monsters.

These minutes, driven by mechanical progressions, monetary objectives, and vital contemplations, have molded the advancement of epic boats and vessels, moving them to phenomenal scales and abilities.

Perhaps of the earliest achievement in sea history that flagged a change in the size of vessels was the development of nautical civic establishments in the old world. The Phoenicians, Egyptians, and Greeks, with their high level route abilities, extended the size and capacities of their boats to work with significant distance exchange and investigation. The interest for bigger vessels emerged from the monetary need of shipping merchandise across tremendous oceanic courses, establishing the groundwork for the sea goliaths that would follow.

The Time of Investigation in the fifteenth and sixteenth hundreds of years denoted a critical defining moment. As European powers set out on aggressive journeys of disclosure, the requirement for vessels fit for overseas travel became evident. The caravel, a profoundly flexibility and secure boat, exemplified the change in transport plan and capacities during this time. These vessels, furnished with cutting edge route instruments, empowered pioneers like Christopher Columbus and Vasco da Gama to navigate huge distances, opening up new oceanic courses and reshaping the worldwide guide.

The seventeenth century saw the coming of tall boats, portrayed by their transcending poles and different sails. The boat of-the-line, furnished with strong cannons, turned into the focal point of maritime armadas during the Time of Sail. This undeniable a change in the capacities of maritime vessels, underlining capability and key predominance. The interest for bigger and all the more intensely furnished ships mirrored the advancing idea of maritime fighting and the essential goals of oceanic powers.

The Modern Upset in the eighteenth and nineteenth hundreds of years achieved extremist changes in oceanic innovation, further enhancing the scale and capacities of boats. The progress from sail to steam power altered impetus, empowering vessels to explore contrary to the natural flow and cross longer distances with sped up and productivity. The presentation of iron and later steel in transport development improved primary trustworthiness, making ready for bigger and more strong vessels.

One of the original crossroads in sea history that undeniable a change in outlook was the improvement of the steamship. The SS Extraordinary England, sent off in 1843, exemplified this groundbreaking time. Planned by Isambard Realm Brunel, the boat joined creative designing with steam impetus, making it the primary maritime vessel with an iron structure and a screw propeller. The SS Extraordinary England not just set new guidelines for size and abilities yet in addition exhibited the capability of steam ability to change sea transportation.

The last 50% of the nineteenth century saw the development of the ironclad warship, an innovative jump that changed maritime capacities. The USS Screen and the CSS Virginia, the two ironclads, conflicted in the Clash of Hampton Streets during the American Nationwide conflict, denoting the primary gathering in battle of shielded warships. This vital second featured the shift from wooden cruising boats to protected vessels, making way for the future improvement of steel-hulled and vigorously outfitted maritime monsters.

The turn of the twentieth century saw the brilliant period of extravagance sea liners, represented by the RMS Titanic and the RMS Sovereign Mary. These goliath vessels, described by extravagant insides and cutting edge conveniences, addressed the peak of traveler transport plan. The interest for bigger and more extravagant liners was driven by the cutthroat idea of overseas travel and the longing to offer travelers unrivaled solace and polish. The sinking of the Titanic in 1912, while a misfortune, provoked a reassessment of security gauges and added to the foundation of sea wellbeing guidelines.

The Second Great War and The Second Great War achieved one more groundbreaking crossroads in oceanic history with the advancement of plane carrying warships. The USS Langley, authorized in 1922, was the main plane carrying warship in the US Naval force. This obvious a change in maritime capacities, stressing the projection of air power adrift. Plane carrying warships, with their capacity to send off and recuperate planes, became crucial parts of current maritime armadas, modifying the elements of maritime fighting and power projection.

The post-The Second Great War time frame saw the coming of containerization, a progressive idea that changed the scale and productivity of oceanic exchange. Malcom McLean's imaginative thought of normalized freight holders, presented during the 1950s, prompted the improvement of compartment ships. These vessels, described by transcending heaps of normalized holders, smoothed out the stacking and dumping processes, decreasing completion times in ports and working with worldwide exchange on a remarkable scale. Containerization denoted a stupendous change in the operations and capacities of sea goliaths, making freight transportation more proficient and savvy.

The late twentieth 100 years and mid 21st century saw the ascent of atomic controlled submarines and surface vessels, addressing a mechanical jump in maritime capacities. The USS Nautilus, authorized in 1954, turned into the world's most memorable functional atomic controlled submarine. Atomic drive furnished submarines with broadened submerged perseverance and vital capacities, modifying the elements of undersea fighting. Plane carrying warships, for example, the USS Undertaking likewise took on atomic power, further upgrading their functional reach and adaptability.

The interest for huge luxury ships, intended for relaxation travel, turned into a characterizing element of the late twentieth 100 years. Journey ships, for example, the Desert garden class vessels, broke records for size and traveler limit.

These drifting hotels, furnished with a horde of conveniences, displayed the voyage business' obligation to furnishing travelers with unmatched diversion and extravagance encounters. The interest for bigger luxury ships mirrored the cutthroat idea of the journey business and the developing notoriety of voyage get-aways.

The investigation of the remote ocean arrived at new wildernesses with the improvement of subs and remotely worked vehicles (ROVs). The Trieste, in 1960, plunged to the Challenger Profound, the most profound point in the sea, denoting a memorable accomplishment in remote ocean investigation. ROVs outfitted with cutting edge sensors and automated capacities took into account maintained and controlled investigation of the sea depths. These mechanical headways extended the scale and abilities of vessels devoted to logical examination and remote ocean investigation.

In late many years, the oceanic business has seen the joining of cutting edge innovations like satellite route, computerized reasoning, and computerization. Worldwide Situating Framework (GPS) innovation, specifically, has changed sea route, giving precise situating information to vessels anyplace on The planet. The interest for vessels furnished with state of the art route frameworks mirrors the business' obligation to improving wellbeing, effectiveness, and situational mindfulness adrift.

The interest for particular vessels custom-made to explicit natural difficulties has acquired conspicuousness in the 21st 100 years. Ice-class vessels intended for Icy route, prepared to deal with outrageous virus conditions, have become fundamental for investigating polar courses and separating assets in the Cold locale. These vessels encapsulate the advancing abilities expected to explore the changing scene of the World's polar areas.

As the sea business advances into the 21st hundred years, a few critical minutes and headways keep on reclassifying the scale and capacities of sea monsters. These extraordinary movements reflect mechanical advancement as well as the developing necessities of worldwide exchange, investigation, and manageability.

The coming of super-sized holder ships addresses a significant defining moment in sea history, displaying the steady quest for productivity and economies of scale. The Triple-E class compartment ships, presented by Maersk Line during the 2010s, represent this pattern. These vessels, known for their huge size and eco-friendliness, have set new guidelines in holder transportation. The interest for bigger compartment ships emerges from the basic to move always expanding volumes of products universally, enhancing coordinated operations and diminishing per-unit transportation costs.

The Panama Channel extension, introduced in 2016, stands apart as a stupendous second that impacted the scale and capacities of oceanic monsters. The development took into account the travel of bigger vessels, known as New Panamax or Neo-Panamax ships, through the trench.

This advancement reshaped worldwide shipping lanes as well as incited the overhaul of vessels to meet the new size limitations of the extended trench. The interest for vessels able to do effectively exploring the extended Panama Trench mirrors the essential significance of this critical stream in worldwide delivery.

The ascent of independent transportation addresses a change in perspective in the capacities of oceanic monsters, as vessels become progressively equipped for working without human mediation. Independent surface vessels (ASVs) and automated submerged vehicles (UUVs) are at the bleeding edge of this mechanical unrest. The interest for independent vessels emerges from the possibility to improve security, lessen functional expenses, and streamline sea strategies through cutting edge man-made brainpower and sensor advances. The arrangement of independent vessels in errands like reconnaissance, information assortment, and natural checking is reshaping the sea scene.

The investigation of seaward environmentally friendly power has led to another interest for vessels intended for the establishment and upkeep of wind turbines and other marine inexhaustible framework. Seaward help vessels, furnished with particular gear and capacities, assume a significant part in the improvement of seaward wind ranches. The interest for vessels equipped for supporting the environmentally friendly power area highlights the oceanic business' obligation to maintainable practices and the change to cleaner energy sources.

The coordination of digitalization and network into oceanic tasks has introduced another period of savvy delivering. The interest for vessels outfitted with Web of Things (IoT) gadgets, information examination, and constant checking frameworks mirrors the business' push towards expanded proficiency, wellbeing, and functional improvement. Brilliant delivery innovations empower vessels to communicate and get information, upgrading navigational capacities, foreseeing upkeep needs, and adding to a more associated and responsive sea environment.

The advancement of maritime abilities go on with the improvement of electromagnetic railguns and coordinated energy weapons. These high level weapon frameworks, which utilize electromagnetic heartbeats or lasers, address a takeoff from conventional maritime cannons. The interest for vessels fit for conveying such state of the art weaponry mirrors the essential basic to remain ahead in maritime fighting and stop expected dangers. The joining of electromagnetic and coordinated energy weapons into sea stages denotes a groundbreaking second in maritime capacities.

The idea of drifting seaward creation units, like drifting melted petroleum gas (FLNG) vessels, has re-imagined the capacities of oceanic monsters in the energy area. These vessels, outfitted with offices for the extraction, handling, and liquefaction of flammable gas, empower the improvement of seaward gas handles that were beforehand monetarily impractical. The interest for FLNG vessels emerges from the need to open new wellsprings of energy and gain by seaward gas saves, extending the compass of the sea business into wilderness energy regions.

The rise of marine advanced mechanics, including submerged drones and remotely worked vehicles (ROVs), has extended the capacities of vessels in the domain of investigation and examination. These automated frameworks consider top to bottom oceanographic studies, submerged investigations, and the investigation of outrageous marine conditions. The interest for vessels furnished with marine mechanical technology mirrors the developing significance of utilizing trend setting innovations to open the secrets of the remote ocean and direct logical examination in already distant regions.

The rising spotlight on supportability and natural obligation has driven the interest for vessels fueled by elective fills and outfitted with cutting edge outflow control innovations. The oceanic business' obligation to decreasing its carbon impression has prompted the improvement of vessels controlled by condensed gaseous petrol (LNG), hydrogen power devices, and, surprisingly, mixture impetus frameworks. The interest for harmless to the ecosystem vessels mirrors a more extensive worldwide familiarity with the natural effect of delivery and the basic to change to greener sea rehearses.

The investigation of the Cold locale for oceanic courses and assets has achieved another interest for ice-class vessels and polar investigation stages. The subsiding ice covers and the launch of the Northern Ocean Course have made the Icy more available, prompting expanded sea exercises in the area. Icebreakers, research vessels, and freight ships intended for polar route mirror the interest for vessels equipped for working in outrageous virus conditions and tending to the difficulties presented by the Cold climate.

The oceanic business keeps on encountering significant minutes that rethink the scale and capacities of sea monsters. From the improvement of super-sized compartment boats to the ascent of independent vessels, every progression mirrors a mix of mechanical development, monetary objectives, and vital contemplations. As the sea scene develops, the interest for vessels will keep on being molded by a unique interaction of variables, including the journey for proficiency, maintainability, and the investigation of new wildernesses. These key minutes address achievements in the continuous story of sea designing, controlling the business toward a future described by development, versatility, and a promise to the dependable utilization of the world's seas.

Chapter 3

Masters of the Sea

"Bosses of the Ocean" typifies the story of sea ability and the unyielding soul of the people who explore the tremendous and flighty seas. The term summons pictures of marine societies, verifiable oceanic accomplishments, and the cutting edge maritime monsters that have formed the course of mankind's set of experiences. This investigation digs into the multi-layered viewpoints that characterize the authority of the ocean, from old sea civilizations to contemporary maritime powers, uncovering the complicated woven artwork of human cooperation with the world's seas.

The foundations of sea authority broaden profound into vestige, where marine societies secured themselves as trailblazers of investigation and exchange. The Phoenicians, eminent sailors of the antiquated Mediterranean, exemplified the dominance of the ocean during the primary thousand years BCE. Their agile and innovatively progressed ships, for example, the kitchen, permitted them to navigate immense distances and lay out shipping lanes that connected the developments of the Eastern Mediterranean. The Phoenicians' oceanic keenness established the groundwork for an organization of sea exchange that molded the social and financial scene of the old world.

In equal, the sea tradition of old Greece unfurled with the appearance of strong maritime city-states, most eminently Athens. The Athenian naval force, instrumental during the Greco-Persian Conflicts, exhibited the essential significance of sea predominance in old fighting. The warship, a spry and intensely equipped warship, turned into an image of maritime dominance, permitting the Athenians to state command over the Aegean Ocean and venture their impact across the Mediterranean. The idea of authority of the ocean in old times rose above simple route; it enveloped military ability, financial essentialness, and social trade.

As history advanced, the Viking sailors arose as experts of the ocean during the Viking Age (eighth to eleventh hundreds of years CE). Hailing from Scandinavia, the Vikings wandered a long ways past their countries, exploring the North Atlantic, the Baltic Ocean, and in any event, coming to the extent that the Mediterranean and the Dark Ocean. Their longships, described by their shallow draft and adaptability, worked with quick attacks, exchange undertakings, and investigation. The Vikings' authority of route, shipbuilding, and seamanship permitted them to explore untamed oceans, waterways, and beach front waters with equivalent artfulness, leaving a getting through engrave on sea history.

The Time of Investigation in the fifteenth and sixteenth hundreds of years denoted a groundbreaking period in the dominance of the ocean. European powers, driven by a journey for new shipping lanes, domains, and wealth, set out on aggressive journeys of revelation. Christopher Columbus, supported by Spain, set out on his noteworthy excursion in 1492, arriving at the Americas and starting another period of overseas investigation. The sea accomplishments of adventurers like Ferdinand Magellan, Vasco da Gama, and John Cabot extended the well explored parts of the planet, preparing for worldwide sea predominance by European countries.

The seventeenth century saw the command of maritime power as a foundation of public strength. The age of the boat of-the-line, impressive warships equipped with various firearm decks, denoted the peak of maritime dominance during the Period of Sail. The maritime competition between European powers, encapsulated by the English Regal Naval force and the French Naval force, assumed a vital part in forming the international affairs of the time. The dominance of maritime strategies, seamanship, and boat configuration became foremost, with the line of fight strategies characterizing commitment between armadas.

Maritime dominance tracked down its apotheosis during the Napoleonic Conflicts, where the Skirmish of Trafalgar in 1805 arose as a pivotal turning point. Chief of naval operations Horatio Nelson, driving the English armada, executed a magnificent system against the joined Franco-Spanish armada. The triumph hardened English maritime matchless quality as well as displayed the essential sharpness and strategic brightness expected for dominance of the ocean. Nelson's renowned sign, "Britain expects that each man will perform his responsibility," resounds as a demonstration of the discipline and expertise innate in sea order.

The Modern Transformation in the eighteenth and nineteenth hundreds of years achieved significant changes in sea innovation, further propelling the dominance of the ocean. The change from sail to steam power altered sea transportation, empowering vessels to explore contrary to the natural flow and navigate longer distances with sped up and proficiency. The advancement of iron and later steel structures upgraded transport strength, sturdiness, and security, laying the foundation for bigger and all the more impressive vessels.

One of the trademark accomplishments of oceanic designing during this period was the development of the SS Extraordinary Eastern, sent off in 1858. Planned by Isambard Realm Brunel, this titanic steamship embodied the aspiration of the period. With a creative blend of screw and paddlewheel drive, the SS Incredible Eastern could oblige great many travelers and convey a lot of freight. In spite of the fact that plagued by monetary difficulties, the vessel addressed a spearheading exertion in pushing the limits of sea innovation and dominance.

The American Nationwide conflict (1861-1865) saw the ascent of ironclad warships, changing maritime fighting and adding to the dominance of the ocean. The USS Screen and the CSS Virginia, the two ironclads, took part in the memorable Clash of Hampton Streets in 1862. This conflict denoted the main gathering in battle of reinforced warships, showing the out of date quality of wooden-hulled vessels notwithstanding high level maritime innovation. The change from sail to steam and the coming of ironclads introduced another time of maritime strength, accentuating the significance of mechanical development in sea technique.

The late nineteenth century saw the prime of extravagance sea liners, typified by the RMS Titanic and her sister ships. These vessels, portrayed by lavish insides and cutting edge conveniences, addressed the exemplification of traveler transport plan and oceanic extravagance. The authority of the ocean, in this specific circumstance, stretched out past route and fighting to envelop the specialty of giving unrivaled solace and style to travelers navigating the overseas course. The sad sinking of the Titanic in 1912, while a human debacle, highlighted the significance of wellbeing and administrative measures in sea tasks.

The Second Great War and The Second Great War saw the finish of maritime power on a worldwide scale. War vessels, plane carrying warships, and submarines turned into the heroes in oceanic battlefields. The Skirmish of Halfway in 1942, a critical showdown between the US and Japan, denoted a defining moment in maritime fighting. Plane carrying warships, exemplified by the USS Undertaking and USS Yorktown, assumed an unequivocal part in the triumph, stressing the essential significance of air power adrift.

The post-The Second Great War time frame introduced the atomic age, with atomic fueled submarines and plane carrying warships becoming images of maritime dominance. The USS Nautilus, charged in 1954, was the world's most memorable functional atomic controlled submarine, displaying the potential for broadened submerged perseverance and key capacities.

Atomic fueled plane carrying warships, like the USS Endeavor, exemplified unmatched functional reach and adaptability, laying out the US as an oceanic superpower.

The last 50% of the twentieth century saw a shift toward expeditionary fighting and power projection capacities. Land and/or water capable attack ships, exemplified by the Wasp-class and America-class vessels, became fundamental parts of present day maritime powers. These vessels, prepared to move and convey Marines and their hardware, displayed the flexibility expected for authority in different oceanic conditions.

The late twentieth century additionally saw the appearance of containerization, changing the scene of worldwide exchange. Compartment ships, for example, the Emma Maersk-class vessels, embody the dominance of operations and effectiveness in sea transport. The normalized freight compartments, presented by Malcom McLean during the 1950s, upset freight taking care of and smoothed out the worldwide inventory network. The dominance of containerization added to the remarkable development of worldwide exchange and reshaped the elements of ports and transportation.

As the world entered the 21st 100 years, the idea of sea authority extended to incorporate arising innovations and international contemplations. Network protection turned into a basic part of maritime tasks, featuring the weakness of interconnected oceanic frameworks to digital dangers. Maritime powers overall put resources into getting their organizations, guaranteeing the strength of correspondence frameworks, and protecting against digital assaults that could think twice about security.

The Cold locale arose as another outskirts, delivering the interest for ice-class vessels fit for exploring polar waters. The retreating ice covers and the launch of the Northern Ocean Course provoked recharged interest in Icy investigation and asset extraction. Icebreakers, research vessels, and freight ships prepared for Icy route became fundamental apparatuses for dominating the difficulties of the super cold and eccentric circumstances in the polar locale.

The 21st century likewise saw a flood in sea mechanical technology and independent frameworks. Automated surface vessels (USVs), submerged drones, and remotely worked vehicles (ROVs) add to the authority of the ocean by empowering maintained and controlled investigation of the sea profundities. These trend setting innovations, outfitted with sensors and mechanical capacities, support logical examination, ecological observing, and submerged reviews, extending the extent of oceanic investigation and information.

In the domain of maritime design, the improvement of covertness innovation has become vital to maritime dominance. Covert plans, for example, those utilized in the Zumwalt-class destroyers, diminish a vessel's radar cross-segment, improving its survivability and lethality in challenged conditions. The authority of secrecy innovation mirrors the continuous weapons contest in maritime abilities, where advancement and mechanical complexity are fundamental.

Contemporary sea authority isn't restricted to maritime powers alone; it reaches out to the expanding field of business space investigation. Privately owned businesses, like SpaceX, have wandered into oceanic activities with independent spaceport drone ships. These robot ships, furnished with dynamic situating frameworks, work with the recuperation of reusable rocket stages adrift, displaying the cooperative energy between sea mastery and space investigation.

The account of "Bosses of the Ocean" winds through the records of mankind's set of experiences, chronicling the advancement of sea dominance from old marine societies to the state of the art innovations of the 21st hundred years. The term incorporates the actual route of the seas as well as the essential sharpness, mechanical development, and flexibility expected to explore the intricacies of the oceanic area. As the world keeps on developing, the dominance of the ocean stays a dynamic and complex undertaking, formed by a conjunction of verifiable inheritances, international contemplations, and the tireless quest for greatness on the world's seas.

3.1 Profiles of the world's largest ships, past and present.

The profiles of the world's biggest boats, over a significant time span, disclose an entrancing excursion through sea designing, mechanical development, and the steadfast quest for pushing the limits of what is conceivable on the high oceans. These titanic vessels, going from noteworthy sea liners to present day supertankers and compartment ships, address the zenith of oceanic accomplishment, each with its interesting story and effect on worldwide exchange and transportation.

One of the famous figures throughout the entire existence of sea goliaths is the RMS Titanic, an extravagance sea liner that graced the waters during the mid twentieth hundred years. Built by the White Star Line, the Titanic was a wonder of designing as well as an image of extravagance and greatness. With a length of roughly 882 feet (268 meters) and a gross weight of around 46,328, the Titanic was the biggest boat above water at the hour of its first venture in 1912. Be that as it may, this superb vessel, promoted as "resilient," unfortunately met its death on its first journey, soaking in the North Atlantic Sea subsequent to crashing into an ice sheet.

In the domain of maritime power, the USS Gerald R. Portage (CVN 78) remains as a contemporary goliath, addressing the zenith of plane carrying warship innovation. Dispatched in 2017, the USS Gerald R. Portage is the lead boat of the Gerald R. Passage class, the US Naval force's most recent class of plane carrying warships. With a length of 1,106 feet (337 meters) and a dislodging of north of 100,000 tons, this atomic fueled supercarrier exhibits cutting edge innovations, including electromagnetic airplane send off frameworks and upgraded flight offices. The USS Gerald R. Portage epitomizes the continuous development of maritime capacities and power projection.

Containerization altered worldwide exchange, and the Emma Maersk-class holder ships encapsulate the scale and effectiveness of present day compartment vessels. The Emma Maersk, sent off in 2006, had a place with a progression of eight sister delivers and held the title of the world's biggest holder transport at the hour of its finish. With a length of 1,302 feet (397 meters) and a conveying limit of more than 15,000 twenty-foot identical units (TEUs), the Emma Maersk set new guidelines for holder transporting. These vessels assume a urgent part in the interconnected trap of the worldwide store network, effectively shipping products across seas.

The Preface FLNG (Drifting Condensed Petroleum gas) becomes the overwhelming focus in the space of drifting creation and storerooms. Worked by Shell, the Introduction FLNG is the biggest seaward office at any point developed. Estimating roughly 1,600 feet (488 meters) long, this drifting behemoth is intended to concentrate, process, and melt flammable gas adrift. Its sheer size and creative way to deal with petroleum gas extraction mark a critical achievement in the use of sea assets and the mission for energy freedom.

The Seawise Monster, initially named the Jahre Viking, holds an unmistakable spot in the chronicles of oceanic history as the biggest boat at any point worked by gross weight. Sent off in 1979 as a supertanker, the Seawise Monster estimated a surprising

1,504 feet (458 meters) long and bragged a gross weight 260,941 tons. Fundamentally utilized for moving unrefined petroleum, this enormous vessel worked during when the interest for huge oil big haulers was at its pinnacle. Its massive size highlighted the mechanical difficulties and designing accomplishments related with developing and overseeing such mammoth boats.

In the space of traveler delivers, the Desert garden class luxury ships, worked by Imperial Caribbean Global, reclassify extravagance and scale in the voyage business. The Desert spring of the Oceans, initiated in 2009, was the primary boat of this class and held the title of the world's biggest voyage transport at the hour of its presentation. With a length of 1,184 feet (361 meters) and a gross weight surpassing 225,000 tons, the Desert garden class vessels are drifting urban communities, including a bunch of conveniences, diversion choices, and facilities for great many travelers. These boats address a combination of sea designing and the neighborliness business, offering travelers an unrivaled journey insight.

In the field of seaward boring, the Berkut stage has a special interest as one of the biggest seaward penetrating stages worldwide. Worked by ExxonMobil, the Berkut stage is arranged in the Arkutun-Dagi field off the shoreline of Sakhalin Island in Russia. Remaining at a level of 482 feet (147 meters) and weighing north of 200,000 tons, this gravity-based structure upholds boring tasks in testing Icy circumstances. The Berkut stage epitomizes the mechanical ability expected to extricate oil and gas from remote and brutal conditions.

The Esso Atlantic and Esso Pacific, known as the "Chadwick D. Viking" big haulers, addressed an earth shattering jump in supertanker plan during the 1970s.

Authorized by ExxonMobil, these vessels estimated 406 meters (1,332 feet) long and held the differentiation of being the principal ULCCs (Ultra Enormous Unrefined Transporters). With a limit of over 3.3 million barrels of oil, these supertankers represented the business' capacity to ship huge amounts of raw petroleum across the world's seas productively.

The Spearheading Soul, a flexible vessel intended for truly difficult work and stage decommissioning, positions among the biggest and most remarkable ships at any point built. Worked by Allseas, the Spearheading Soul brags a length 1,253 feet (382 meters) and elements a novel twin-hulled plan. Outfitted with a cutting edge lifting framework, this super vessel can lift and ship whole seaward oil and gas stages, smoothing out decommissioning endeavors in the North Ocean. The Spearheading Soul represents the inventiveness expected to address the difficulties of the seaward energy industry.

The Maersk Triple-E class compartment ships, representing the standards of Economy of scale, Energy productivity, and Naturally further developed execution, feature the following boondocks in holder delivering. Sent off in 2013, the Triple-E class vessels, including the Mary Maersk and her sister ships, rank among the biggest holder ships in activity. With a length of 1,312 feet (400 meters) and a limit of around

18,000 TEUs, these boats typify the business' obligation to maintainability, including progressed energy-saving innovations and harmless to the ecosystem plan standards.

The Preface FLNG (Drifting Condensed Petroleum gas) becomes the overwhelming focus in the area of drifting creation and storage spaces. Worked by Shell, the Introduction FLNG is the biggest seaward office at any point built. Estimating around 1,600 feet (488 meters) long, this drifting behemoth is intended to concentrate, process, and condense flammable gas adrift. Its sheer size and creative way to deal with petroleum gas extraction mark a huge achievement in the usage of sea assets and the mission for energy freedom.

The profiles of these epic vessels, traversing various periods and oceanic areas, by and large portray the account of humankind's journey to overcome the oceans and saddle their true capacity. From the glory of extravagance liners to the proficiency of compartment ships and the specialized wonders of seaward stages, every vessel addresses a part in the continuous adventure of oceanic development. These boats, over a significant time span, stand as demonstration of the unstoppable human soul, stretching the boundaries of what can be accomplished on the world's seas. As the oceanic business keeps on developing, these profiles act as markers of the achievements came to, the difficulties survive, and the vast potential outcomes that lie ahead in the steadily extending area of the world's biggest boats.

3.2 Detailed narratives of their construction, maiden voyages, and notable accomplishments.

The development, first trips, and striking achievements of the world's biggest boats give a definite story of human resourcefulness, oceanic designing, and the extraordinary effect these vessels have had on worldwide exchange, transportation, and investigation. Every one of these oceanic monsters, crossing different periods and purposes, has a special story to tell, mirroring the mechanical headways and difficulties of now is the ideal time.

The RMS Titanic, frequently inseparable from misfortune, had a development that reflected the richness and loftiness of the mid twentieth 100 years. Imagined as a feature of the White Star Line's Olympic-class threesome, close by the RMS Britannic and RMS Olympic, the Titanic's development started in 1909 at the Harland and Wolff shipyard in Belfast, Ireland. The boat's plan integrated the most recent security highlights, including watertight compartments and electrically worked watertight entryways. The Titanic's sheer size was a wonder, extending roughly 882 feet (268 meters) long and bragging a gross weight around 46,328.

The Titanic's first trip started on April 10, 1912, from Southampton, Britain, with stops in Cherbourg, France, and Queenstown (presently Cobh), Ireland, prior to heading across the Atlantic to New York City. The journey was set apart by a mix of cultural classes ready, from the lavish top notch facilities to the more unassuming quarters of the second rate class. Sadly, the boat's unfortunate experience with an ice shelf on April 14, 1912, brought about its sinking, prompting the deficiency of north of 1,500 lives.

As a conspicuous difference to the Titanic's destiny, the USS Gerald R. Passage (CVN 78), the lead boat of the Gerald R. Passage class of plane carrying warships, left on a memorable excursion of maritime development. The development of the USS Gerald R. Portage started in 2005 at the Newport News Shipbuilding in Virginia, USA. This atomic fueled supercarrier was imagined as a jump forward in maritime capacities, consolidating trend setting innovations, for example, the Electromagnetic Airplane Send off Framework (EMALS) and the High level Capturing Stuff (AAG). With a length of 1,106 feet (337 meters) and a dislodging surpassing 100,000 tons, the USS Gerald R. Passage addresses the bleeding edge of maritime designing.

The USS Gerald R. Passage's first trip occurred on July 22, 2017, following its appointing prior that month. The boat went through a progression of ocean preliminaries to test its different frameworks and capacities, denoting a vital stage in its functional preparation. The effective sending of these trend setting innovations on the USS Gerald R. Passage has not just set another norm for plane carrying warships yet in addition underlined the US Naval force's obligation to keeping up with maritime predominance.

Containerization, an upheaval in worldwide exchange, found its exemplification in the Emma Maersk-class compartment ships, with the Emma Maersk driving the armada. Built by the Odense Steel Shipyard in Denmark, the Emma Maersk was sent off in 2006 as the first of a progression of eight sister ships. The boat's plan focused on effectiveness, with a length of 1,302 feet (397 meters) and a conveying limit outperforming 15,000 twenty-foot comparable units (TEUs). The Emma Maersk and her sister ships were crucial in reshaping the scene of sea operations, enhancing the transportation of merchandise across seas.

The Emma Maersk's first trip started in 2006, and it quickly procured acknowledgment as the biggest holder transport on the planet around then. The organization of these gigantic vessels denoted a change in perspective in compartment delivering, underscoring economies of scale and the smoothing out of freight dealing with processes. The Emma Maersk's remarkable achievement lies in its job as an impetus for the improvement of super compartment ships, encouraging expanded proficiency and cost-viability in the worldwide store network.

In the space of seaward energy, the Preface FLNG (Drifting Condensed Gaseous petrol) arose as a momentous task. The development of the Preface FLNG occurred at the Samsung Weighty Ventures shipyard in South Korea. The vessel, dispatched by Shell, introduced an original way to deal with petroleum gas extraction by empowering the handling and liquefaction of gas adrift. Estimating roughly 1,600 feet (488 meters) long, the Introduction FLNG turned into the biggest seaward office at any point built.

The Preface FLNG's first venture started in late 2017 when it was towed from the building site to its working area off the shoreline of Western Australia. This weighty vessel denoted a change in the seaward energy industry, offering an adaptable and financially savvy answer for separating and handling flammable gas in far off areas.

The Preface FLNG's eminent achievement lies in its capacity to open already blocked off seaward gas saves, adding to the worldwide energy supply.

The Seawise Monster, initially known as the Jahre Viking, left a mark on the world as the biggest boat at any point worked by gross weight. Built by Sumitomo Weighty Businesses in Japan, the supertanker estimated a bewildering 1,504 feet (458 meters) long and had a gross weight of 260,941 tons. Sent off in 1979, the Seawise Monster was principally utilized for moving unrefined petroleum and represented the interest for gigantic oil big haulers during that time.

The Seawise Goliath's first venture denoted the start of its administration in the worldwide oil transportation industry. Its outstanding achievement lies in its functional limit, having moved large number of barrels of raw petroleum across the world's seas during its dynamic years. The vessel's tremendous size highlighted the strategic and designing difficulties related with overseeing such mammoth ships and mirrored the business' drive to satisfy the needs of the developing worldwide oil market.

In the domain of traveler sends, the Desert garden class luxury ships, including the Desert spring of the Oceans, set new principles for extravagance and scale in the journey business. Built by the STX Europe shipyard in Turku, Finland, the Desert spring of the Oceans was sent off in 2009. With a length of 1,184 feet (361 meters) and a gross weight surpassing 225,000 tons, the Desert garden of the Oceans turned into the world's biggest journey transport at the hour of its introduction.

The Desert spring of the Oceans left on its first venture in December 2009, offering travelers an unmatched voyage insight. The boat's creative plan included unmistakable areas, a Focal Park with living vegetation, and different diversion choices, rethinking the idea of cruising for a great scope. The Desert garden class luxury ships' prominent achievement lies in their capacity to give a vivid and different scope of encounters for huge number of travelers, setting another benchmark for the journey business.

In the space of seaward boring, the Berkut stage, situated in the Arkutun-Dagi field off the shore of Sakhalin Island in Russia, addresses a zenith in penetrating stage development. The Berkut stage, worked by ExxonMobil, was developed at the Kola Shipyard in Murmansk, Russia. Remaining at a level of 482 feet (147 meters) and weighing more than 200,000 tons, this gravity-based structure upholds boring tasks in testing Cold circumstances.

The Berkut stage's remarkable achievement lies in its fruitful sending for seaward boring in the unforgiving Cold climate. The stage's development and functional capacities highlight the business' capacity to extricate significant assets from remote and testing areas. The Berkut stage represents the joining of cutting edge designing answers for explore outrageous circumstances and add to the worldwide energy supply.

The Esso Atlantic and Esso Pacific, known as the "Chadwick D. Viking" big haulers, introduced another period in supertanker plan during the 1970s. Appointed by ExxonMobil, these vessels estimated 406 meters (1,332 feet) long, making them the primary Ultra Huge Rough Transporters (ULCCs). With a limit of over 3.3 million barrels of oil, these supertankers represented the business' capacity to ship tremendous amounts of raw petroleum across the world's seas proficiently.

The Esso Atlantic and Esso Pacific set out on their launches as spearheading vessels in the domain of oil transportation. Their remarkable achievement lies in their job as pioneers in the time of super huge big haulers, adding to the proficient and practical development of unrefined petroleum on a worldwide scale. These supertankers addressed a reaction to the rising interest for oil transportation and exhibited the business' obligation to development in vessel plan.

The Spearheading Soul, worked by Allseas, remains as a demonstration of the capacities of present day oceanic designing. Developed at the Daewoo Shipbuilding and Marine Designing (DSME) shipyard in South Korea, the Spearheading Soul has a length of 1,253 feet (382 meters) and highlights an exceptional twin-hulled plan.

The vessel is outfitted with a cutting edge lifting framework equipped for eliminating whole seaward oil and gas stages, smoothing out decommissioning endeavors in the North Ocean.

The Spearheading Soul's first journey in 2016 denoted a critical progression in seaward stage decommissioning. Its striking achievement lies in its unrivaled lifting limit, which considers the expulsion of huge designs in a solitary piece, diminishing the natural effect of decommissioning exercises. The Spearheading Soul addresses a change in outlook in the seaward energy industry, displaying the coordination of trend setting innovation to address complex difficulties.

The Maersk Triple-E class holder ships, including the Mary Maersk and her sister ships, represent the following boondocks in compartment transporting. Developed by the Daewoo Shipbuilding and Marine Designing (DSME) shipyard in South Korea, the Triple-E class vessels were sent off in 2013. With a length of 1,312 feet (400 meters) and a limit of around 18,000 TEUs, these boats represent the business' obligation to manageability, highlighting progressed energy-saving innovations and harmless to the ecosystem plan standards.

The Maersk Triple-E class vessels set out on their launches as a reaction to the developing interest for more manageable compartment delivering. Their remarkable achievement lies in their execution of creative highlights, for example, a twin-screw plan, which improves eco-friendliness and lessens natural effect. The Triple-E class vessels address an amicable harmony between financial proficiency, energy preservation, and natural obligation in the worldwide transportation industry.

The stories of development, launches, and outstanding achievements of the world's biggest boats weave an embroidery of sea history, mirroring the advancement of human capacities and goals on the oceans. From the magnificence of extravagance liners to the proficiency of holder sends, every vessel epitomizes the soul of now is the right time, pushing the limits of what is feasible on the huge field of the world's seas. These stories annal mechanical progressions as well as feature the dauntless human soul that keeps on pushing the oceanic business toward new skylines.

3.3 Insights into the roles these vessels play in various industries, from shipping to exploration.

The world's biggest boats assume different and significant parts across a range of businesses, adding to worldwide exchange, investigation, asset extraction, and mechanical development. Every one of these monster vessels is carefully designed to satisfy the needs of explicit businesses, displaying the flexibility and adaptability of oceanic designing. From compartment ships working with the development of merchandise to seaward stages empowering oil and gas extraction, the jobs these vessels play are basic to the working of the advanced world.

Holder ships, exemplified by the Emma Maersk-class vessels, assume a focal part in the worldwide delivery industry, filling in as the foundation of global exchange. These mammoth vessels are intended to move normalized freight holders, empowering proficient stacking and dumping at ports around the world. The Emma Maersk, with its length of 1,302 feet (397 meters) and a limit surpassing 15,000 twenty-foot comparable units (TEUs), addresses the embodiment of compartment transport proficiency.

The job of compartment ships is major to the interconnected idea of the worldwide economy. They work with the transportation of products across seas, connecting makers with purchasers, and adding to the consistent progression of wares. The normalized compartments, presented during the twentieth hundred years, reformed freight dealing with, diminishing stacking and dumping times and upgrading the general productivity of sea transportation.

The meaning of holder ships is apparent in their effect on worldwide exchange designs. They have empowered the globalization of supply chains, permitting organizations to source materials and items from various areas of the planet. The productivity and cost-viability of holder delivering have added to the development of cross-country exchange, forming the elements of the assembling and retail areas. These vessels, with their tremendous freight limits, typify the monetary standard of economies of scale, making worldwide exchange more open and reasonable.

In the domain of seaward energy, drifting creation and storage spaces, like the Preface FLNG (Drifting Condensed Petroleum gas), assume an essential part in the extraction and handling of flammable gas. Developed by Shell, the Preface FLNG is the biggest seaward office at any point assembled, estimating roughly 1,600 feet (488 meters) long. Its essential job is to separate petroleum gas from seaward fields, process it ready, and condense it for transportation.

The Introduction FLNG's job stretches out past customary seaward stages, offering an adaptable and practical answer for getting to remote gas holds. Its capacity to work in seaward conditions dispenses with the requirement for fixed foundation, lessening the ecological effect and empowering the improvement of fields that would be trying to take advantage of utilizing regular strategies. The Introduction FLNG embodies the development of seaward energy advances, opening new boondocks for the investigation and extraction of regular assets.

Supertankers, similar to the Seawise Monster (previously Jahre Viking), are vital to the worldwide oil industry, working with the transportation of unrefined petroleum from oil-delivering locales to treatment facilities around the world. The Seawise Monster, with its length of 1,504 feet (458 meters) and a gross weight of 260,941 tons, worked during a time of popularity for monstrous oil big haulers. Its job was to proficiently ship huge amounts of unrefined petroleum across seas, connecting oil-delivering countries with significant utilization habitats.

The job of supertankers is urgent in guaranteeing a consistent and solid stockpile of unrefined petroleum to meet the energy needs of countries all over the planet. These vessels explore significant ocean courses, navigating the seas to convey oil to treatment facilities that cycle it into different oil based commodities. The effective transportation of raw petroleum by supertankers is a foundation of the worldwide energy framework, empowering the working of businesses, transportation frameworks, and families that depend on petrol based items.

In the journey business, Desert garden class luxury ships, including the Desert garden of the Oceans, assume an extraordinary part in reclassifying the idea of extravagance travel and diversion adrift. Developed by the STX Europe shipyard, the Desert garden of the Oceans, with its length of 1,184 feet (361 meters) and a gross weight surpassing 225,000 tons, addresses the zenith of journey transport plan. The job of these luxury ships is to furnish travelers with a complex and vivid experience, offering a drifting city with a bunch of conveniences and diversion choices.

The job of Desert garden class luxury ships stretches out past ordinary voyage encounters, embracing the idea of a drifting hotel. These vessels take care of a different scope of inclinations and interests, highlighting particular areas, theaters, cafés, shopping regions, and, surprisingly, open air parks. The job of these luxury ships is to establish an independent and extravagant climate, where travelers can partake in a wide exhibit of exercises while venturing out to various locations.

In seaward boring, stages like the Berkut stage assume a basic part in removing oil and gas from underneath the sea floor. Situated in the Arkutun-Dagi field off the shore of Sakhalin Island in Russia, the Berkut stage remains at a level of 482 feet (147 meters) and weighs north of 200,000 tons. Its essential job is to help penetrating activities in testing Icy circumstances, adding to the investigation and extraction of seaward hydrocarbon assets.

The job of seaward penetrating stages is fundamental in opening the capability of seaward oil and gas saves. These designs house boring gear, extraction offices, and residing quarters for the faculty engaged with penetrating activities. The job of the Berkut stage, working in the Icy, features the business' capacity to adjust to outrageous ecological circumstances and highlights the essential significance of seaward investigation in satisfying worldwide energy needs.

Ultra Enormous Rough Transporters (ULCCs), addressed by the Esso Atlantic and Esso Pacific, play had a notable impact in the transportation of raw petroleum on a remarkable scale. Dispatched by ExxonMobil, these vessels, estimating 406 meters

(1,332 feet) long, were the first of their sort and represented a jump forward in super-tanker plan. Their job was to effectively move tremendous amounts of unrefined petroleum across the world's seas, fulfilling the rising need for oil during the 1970s.

The job of ULCCs in the oil business is vital in guaranteeing the convenient and practical transportation of raw petroleum from oil-delivering areas to treatment facilities. These vessels work on major sea courses, exploring through seas to convey fundamental energy assets. The job of the Esso Atlantic and Esso Pacific in the advancement of oil transportation exhibits the business' obligation to development and proficiency in gathering the world's energy needs.

The Spearheading Soul, worked by Allseas, rethinks the job of vessels in the seaward business by having some expertise in hard work and stage decommissioning. Built at the Daewoo Shipbuilding and Marine Designing (DSME) shipyard, the Spearheading Soul has a length of 1,253 feet (382 meters) and elements an exceptional twin-hulled plan. Its job is to lift and ship whole seaward oil and gas stages, smoothing out decommissioning endeavors in the North Ocean.

The job of the Spearheading Soul is instrumental in tending to the difficulties of decommissioning maturing seaward framework. By lifting whole stages in a solitary piece, the vessel limits the natural effect of decommissioning exercises and improves the usage of assets. The job of this uber vessel mirrors the business' obligation to capable practices and mechanical advancement in dealing with the lifecycle of seaward establishments.

The Maersk Triple-E class compartment ships, including the Mary Maersk and her sister ships, embrace a job that goes past traditional holder transporting by integrating maintainability and energy productivity. Developed by the Daewoo Shipbuilding and Marine Designing (DSME) shipyard, these vessels have a length of 1,312 feet (400 meters) and a limit of around 18,000 TEUs. Their job is to move products while focusing on ecological contemplations and energy protection.

The job of the Triple-E class holder ships lines up with the business' developing accentuation on manageability and green practices. These vessels highlight cutting edge innovations, for example, a twin-screw plan and a waste intensity recuperation framework, to decrease fuel utilization and emanations. The job of the Mary Maersk and her sister ships mirrors a pledge to offsetting financial effectiveness with ecological obligation in the worldwide delivery industry.

The world's biggest boats assume essential parts in forming different ventures, affecting worldwide exchange, energy extraction, and relaxation travel. From compartment ships working with the development of products to seaward stages supporting oil and gas investigation, every vessel is a demonstration of human development and flexibility on the high oceans. These oceanic monsters not just add to the working of individual businesses yet additionally assume interconnected parts in the unpredictable snare of the advanced worldwide economy. As ventures advance and needs shift, these gigantic vessels keep on adjusting, exhibiting their getting through importance in the powerful scene of sea exercises.

The jobs of the world's biggest boats expand further into the domains of mechanical advancement, ecological contemplations, and key international relations, mirroring the unique scene of the oceanic business. As these huge vessels explore the oceans, they epitomize a combination of designing ability, manageability drives, and reactions to international goals.

One of the eminent perspectives molding the job of the world's biggest boats is the mix of cutting edge innovations. The oceanic business has embraced computerization, digitalization, and man-made consciousness to improve vessel execution, wellbeing, and functional proficiency. Compartment ships, exemplified by the Maersk Triple-E class, have become stages for development, integrating shrewd advances that improve course arranging, fuel utilization, and support plans.

The job of innovation in these vessels stretches out past functional effectiveness to address natural worries. As the worldwide local area wrestles with the effect of environmental change, there is a developing accentuation on the job of the oceanic business in lessening its carbon impression. The Global Sea Association (IMO) has set aggressive focuses to decarbonize the area, inciting the improvement of eco-accommodating advancements for impetus, energy proficiency, and elective energizes.

The Maersk Triple-E class compartment ships represent this pattern, including plan components zeroed in on supportability. The vessels utilize a twin-screw plan to further develop eco-friendliness, and their waste intensity recuperation framework changes over exhaust heat into extra impetus power. These developments mirror a more extensive industry obligation to relieving natural effect and progressing reasonable practices in oceanic transportation.

In the seaward energy area, the job of uber vessels stretches out to tending to the difficulties of environmentally friendly power advancement. Seaward wind ranches, situated in oceanic conditions, require specific vessels for the establishment and support of wind turbines. Here, vessels like the Spearheading Soul show their adaptability, adding to the development of environmentally friendly power by supporting the development of seaward wind framework.

The Spearheading Soul's lifting limit and dynamic situating capacities make it an important resource for the establishment of enormous breeze turbine parts in testing marine conditions. Its part in the seaward wind area lines up with the more extensive worldwide push toward sustainable power sources, exhibiting how sea monsters add to the energy progress and the decrease of dependence on customary petroleum products.

As the jobs of these vessels advance, international contemplations likewise become possibly the most important factor. The essential significance of ocean courses, sea chokepoints, and admittance to normal assets impacts the job and sending of huge boats.

The Cold district, once out of reach because of ice cover, has turned into a point of convergence for oceanic exercises with the subsiding ice covers. Ice-class vessels, equipped for exploring polar waters, assume an essential part in Icy investigation and asset extraction.

The Seawise Monster, initially known as the Jahre Viking, saw a changing international scene during its functional years. Its job in moving unrefined petroleum across worldwide waters was entwined with international occasions that formed the oil business. Admittance to oceanic courses, for example, the Waterway of Hormuz and the Suez Channel, has been a point of convergence of international pressures, underscoring the essential job of vessels in getting energy supply chains.

The Icy, with its immense undiscovered assets, has accumulated expanded consideration, prompting the advancement of ice-class vessels like the Christophe de Margerie, an icebreaking LNG transporter. These vessels assume a basic part in working with Icy transportation courses and getting to normal assets in the district. As the Cold turns out to be more open, the job of ice-class vessels in exploring these difficult waters is critical for financial and vital interests.

Besides, the oceanic business converges with the thriving field of business space investigation. Sea tasks currently stretch out past Earth's air, with privately owned businesses wandering into space exercises. SpaceX, established by Elon Musk, epitomizes this crossing point with its independent spaceport drone ships. These vessels, outfitted with dynamic situating frameworks, assume a vital part in the recuperation of reusable rocket stages adrift.

The job of sea skill in space tasks features the cooperative energy among oceanic and space businesses. Independent spaceport drone ships feature the flexibility of sea advancements in assorted conditions, from the sea surface to the vacuum of room. As space investigation keeps on propelling, the job of oceanic monsters in supporting space exercises is probably going to develop, building up the interconnected idea of these areas.

The account of the world's biggest ships likewise envelops the job of maritime powers in shielding oceanic security. Past their customary jobs in safeguard, maritime vessels are presently furnished with cutting edge innovations to address arising dangers in the digital space. Network protection has turned into a basic part of sea tasks, taking into account the weakness of interconnected frameworks to digital dangers.

The USS Gerald R. Passage, an innovative wonder among plane carrying warships, represents the development of maritime capacities into the domain of network protection. Its job goes past regular power projection to incorporate getting organizations, guaranteeing correspondence versatility, and safeguarding against digital assaults. The mix of online protection measures mirrors the contemporary difficulties looked by maritime powers in a period of computerized interconnectedness.

The world's biggest boats, through their different jobs and crossing points with innovation, manageability, international affairs, and security, highlight the intricacy of the sea space. They explore actual oceans as well as the flows of monetary, political, and mechanical change. As the oceanic business keeps on developing, these titanic vessels will assume basic parts in molding the fate of worldwide exchange, energy, and investigation. Their jobs reach out into the great beyond, denoting the boondocks of human accomplishment on the tremendous material of the world's seas.

Chapter 4

Conquering the Depths

Overcoming the profundities of the world's seas has been a persevering through human mission, driven by a blend of logical interest, mechanical development, and financial open door. As we dive into the investigation of the deep domains, a significant excursion unfurls, uncovering the difficulties, disclosures, and extraordinary innovations that have denoted the triumph of the sea profundities.

The investigation of the remote ocean is intrinsically attached to the human tendency for revelation. From old fantasies and legends that discussed strange ocean animals hiding in the profundities to the logical interest that arose during the Renaissance, the sea has consistently held a persona that coaxed investigation. Early endeavors to comprehend the profundities included simple subs and jumping ringers, giving restricted looks into the secretive submerged world.

The nineteenth century saw critical steps in remote ocean investigation, with the appearance of specific hardware and procedures. The HMS Challenger, an English Imperial Naval force transport, set out on a pivotal logical endeavor from 1872 to 1876.

Furnished with sounding hardware, fishes, and water testing gadgets, the Challenger campaign planned the sea depths, distinguished marine life, and gathered important information that established the groundwork for current oceanography.

During the twentieth 100 years, the investigation of the sea profundities took a goliath jump forward with the improvement of submarines equipped for conveying people into the void. The Bathyscaphe Trieste, planned by Swiss architect Auguste Piccard and worked in a joint effort with the US Naval force, left a mark on the world in 1960 by dropping to the Challenger Profound, the most profound point on the planet's seas. Steered by Jacques Piccard and Wear Walsh, the Trieste arrived at a profundity of around 35,797 feet (10,911 meters), opening another part in humankind's success of the remote ocean.

The resulting many years saw the refinement of sub advances and the foundation of examination organizations devoted to remote ocean investigation. Alvin, a remote ocean submarine worked by the Forest Opening Oceanographic Organization, turned into a spearheading vessel, making various jumps and adding to disclosures, for example, remote ocean aqueous vents and the destruction of the Titanic.

As mechanical progressions sped up, remotely worked vehicles (ROVs) and independent submerged vehicles (AUVs) arose as vital devices for investigating the sea profundities. ROVs, fastened to surface vessels, considered exact moving and the assortment of tests from outrageous profundities. AUVs, then again, worked independently, covering immense regions of the sea floor and directing itemized studies.

The investigation of aqueous vents, found in the late twentieth hundred years, reformed how we might interpret life in outrageous conditions. These vents, situated along mid-sea edges, discharge mineral-rich liquids that help interesting environments overflowing with beforehand obscure species. The revelation tested customary thoughts of life's reliance on daylight and exhibited the strength of living things adjusted to the brutal states of the remote ocean.

Mechanical advancements in materials science, mechanical technology, and imaging play played critical parts in growing our capacities to investigate the sea profundities. Superior quality cameras, sent on submarines and ROVs, give exceptional clearness in catching pictures and recordings of the remote ocean climate. Modern sonar frameworks empower itemized planning of the sea depths, uncovering undersea elements like seamounts, channels, and geographical arrangements.

The advancement of remotely worked vehicles with controller arms has empowered researchers to lead perplexing analyses and gather tests from the remote ocean floor.

These ROVs, furnished with cutting edge imaging frameworks, permit specialists to concentrate on marine life right at home, revealing insight into the ways of behaving and transformations of species in the outrageous tensions and haziness of the profound sea.

One of the astounding revelations worked with by remote ocean investigation is the recognizable proof of bioluminescent organic entities that populate the profundities. Bioluminescence, the capacity of living creatures to deliver light, is a broad peculiarity in the remote ocean, serving different environmental capabilities, for example, drawing in prey, hindering hunters, and working with correspondence without a trace of daylight. The investigation of bioluminescent creatures has extended how we might interpret sea life science as well as enlivened developments in biotechnology and clinical imaging.

The investigation of the sea profundities isn't bound to logical undertakings alone; it stretches out to financial exercises with the revelation of significant assets in the deep locales. Remote ocean mining, an early industry, plans to extricate minerals, for example, polymetallic knobs, polymetallic sulfides, and cobalt-rich ferromanganese hulls from the sea depths. These minerals, wealthy in metals like copper, nickel, and uncommon earth components, hold potential for satisfying the developing need for unrefined substances in different businesses.

While remote ocean mining presents financial open doors, it likewise raises worries about its natural effect on delicate environments. The likely interruption to remote ocean territories and the dubious results of extricating minerals from the sea floor have provoked calls for worldwide guidelines and manageable practices to administer this arising industry. Finding some kind of harmony between monetary turn of events and natural protection stays a vital test in the continuous success of the sea profundities.

The deep fields, described by immense regions of level, dregs covered seabed, address quite possibly of the least investigated environment on The planet. Regardless of their apparently tedious appearance, deep fields harbor different and novel living things adjusted to the outrageous states of the remote ocean. The investigation of these fields has uncovered an abundance of biodiversity, including confounding species like remote ocean jellyfish, monster isopods, and slippery cephalopods.

The Mariana Channel, home to the Challenger Profound, remains as a definitive outskirts in remote ocean investigation. Arranged in the western Pacific Sea, the channel arrives at stunning profundities of more than 36,000 feet (10,994 meters). The investigation of the Mariana Channel includes defeating gigantic tensions, outrageous temperatures, and specialized difficulties related with arriving at the most profound point on earth.

James Cameron, the prestigious movie producer and voyager, plummeted into the Challenger Somewhere down in 2012 in the sub Deepsea Challenger.

His independent campaign denoted a notable accomplishment, displaying the innovative capacities that permit people to arrive at the most profound openings of the sea. The information and tests gathered during the endeavor add to continuous logical exploration pointed toward opening the secrets of the Mariana Channel.

The investigation of the sea profundities has likewise disclosed the interconnectedness of marine environments and the significant impact of the remote ocean on worldwide environment guideline. Remote ocean flows, driven by temperature and saltiness slopes, assume a urgent part in the sea's course designs. The ingestion of carbon dioxide by remote ocean waters mitigates the effects of environmental change by managing climatic carbon levels.

Besides, the remote ocean goes about as a repository for microbial life that assumes a crucial part in biogeochemical cycles. Microorganisms in the remote ocean climate add to supplement cycling, carbon sequestration, and the debasement of natural matter. Understanding the microbial networks in the remote ocean gives bits of knowledge into the key cycles that support life on The planet and impact the wellbeing of the planet.

The mission to overcome the profundities of the sea additionally includes the quest for extraterrestrial life. The outrageous states of the remote ocean, with its shortfall of daylight, high tensions, and one of a kind biological systems, act as analogs for conditions on other heavenly bodies, like Jupiter's moon Europa or Saturn's moon

Enceladus. Researchers guess that subsurface seas on these moons could hold onto conditions helpful for life, and concentrating on Earth's remote ocean conditions gives important experiences to future investigation missions.

As we keep on unwinding the secrets of the sea profundities, moral contemplations become progressively relevant. The sensitive equilibrium of remote ocean biological systems, the possible effects of human exercises, and the safeguarding of biodiversity request cautious moral investigation. The standard of mindful stewardship highlights the significance of reasonable practices in remote ocean investigation, guaranteeing that our mission for information doesn't think twice about respectability of the sea's environments.

The victory of the sea profundities addresses a multi-faceted excursion incorporating logical disclosure, mechanical development, monetary potential, and moral obligation. From the beginning of speculative investigation to the state of the art subs and mechanical technology of today, mankind's commitment with the remote ocean has advanced, uncovering the marvels and intricacies of this secret domain. The continuous investigation of the deep profundities holds guarantee for additional disclosures about the starting points of life, the elements of Earth's environment, and the potential for extraterrestrial tenability. As we explore the unfamiliar waters of the remote ocean, the journey to overcome its profundities mirrors our persevering through interest and the aggregate human undertaking to grasp the secrets that lie underneath the outer layer of the world's seas.

4.1 Exploration of how modern maritime technology enables the construction of massive vessels capable of navigating deep oceans.

The development of enormous vessels equipped for exploring profound seas is a demonstration of the collaboration between present day oceanic innovation, designing development, and the steady quest for pushing the limits of what is feasible on the high oceans. In investigating the wonders of contemporary oceanic innovation, we reveal the many-sided processes, state of the art materials, and modern plan rules that meet up to make epic boats equipped for crossing the world's most profound and most testing waters.

At the core of current oceanic innovation lies the workmanship and study of maritime design. Maritime draftsmen are entrusted with planning vessels that not just endure the powers of the untamed sea yet in addition improve execution, eco-friendliness, and security. PC supported plan (computer aided design) has altered the field, permitting engineers to make profoundly nitty gritty and exact virtual models of boats before the actual development starts. This iterative plan process empowers the advancement of body shapes, hydrodynamics, and generally speaking underlying honesty.

The development of materials utilized in shipbuilding is a foundation of current sea innovation. Conventional materials like steel stay fundamental, giving the strength and toughness essential for marine vessels. Be that as it may, headways in materials science have presented high-strength amalgams, lightweight composites, and even fiber-built up plastics. These materials add to the development of vessels that are hearty as well as show further developed eco-friendliness and erosion opposition.

Consider the Maersk Triple-E class holder ships as a great representation of how current materials upgrade sea capacities. Developed utilizing high-strength steel combinations, these vessels are intended for both underlying uprightness and functional proficiency. The utilization of cutting edge materials takes into account the formation of bigger, more smoothed out bodies that diminish drag, at last further developing eco-friendliness and lessening natural effect.

The drive frameworks of present day oceanic monsters are a zenith of designing development. While conventional impetus techniques, for example, diesel motors, keep on driving numerous vessels, there is a developing movement towards option and more reasonable arrangements. Coordinated power the executives frameworks, energy-effective propellers, and the investigation of electric and half and half impetus advances embody the state of the art improvements in this domain.

With regards to drive, consider the progressions in the voyage business with the presentation of the Desert spring class luxury ships. These vessels use a blend of diesel-electric impetus and azimuth unit drives, considering upgraded mobility and eco-friendliness.

The coordination of cutting edge drive frameworks not just works on the natural impression of these titanic ships yet additionally raises the general journey insight for travelers.

The execution of cutting edge route and control frameworks is one more element of present day oceanic innovation. Satellite route, dynamic situating frameworks, and high level radar and sonar innovations engage vessels to explore with unrivaled accuracy, guaranteeing safe section through unpredictable streams and testing conditions. Mechanized frameworks additionally add to the functional proficiency of boats, decreasing the responsibility on the team and upgrading in general wellbeing.

In the seaward energy area, investigation and creation stages influence current oceanic innovation for exact situating and dependability. The Berkut stage, arranged in the difficult Cold climate off the shore of Sakhalin Island in Russia, embodies the coordination of cutting edge route and control frameworks. The stage's dynamic situating capacities empower it to keep a steady situation for boring tasks regardless of the brutal natural circumstances, exhibiting how innovation empowers seaward exercises in beforehand difficult to reach locales.

The coming of digitalization and the Web of Things (IoT) has introduced another time of availability and information driven dynamic in oceanic tasks. Shrewd sensors and observing frameworks are inserted all through vessels to gather continuous information on different boundaries, including motor execution, fuel utilization, and ecological circumstances. This information is then broke down to improve functional proficiency, perform prescient upkeep, and upgrade in general security.

In the holder delivering industry, the Maersk Triple-E class vessels use progressed information examination to screen and improve execution. The combination of sensors all through the boat takes into consideration the continuous following of freight conditions, fuel utilization, and motor execution. This information driven approach not just works on the functional productivity of the vessel yet in addition works with informed decision-production for course arranging and upkeep planning.

In the domain of seaward boring, remotely worked vehicles (ROVs) furnished with cutting edge sensors and cameras have become crucial devices for subsea investigation and upkeep. These ROVs, controlled from the surface, give ongoing symbolism and information from the sea floor, permitting administrators to evaluate the state of subsea framework and arrive at informed conclusions about upkeep and fixes.

The plan standards of current sea innovation likewise focus on ecological manageability. As the oceanic business faces expanding investigation for its natural effect, shipbuilders and administrators are effectively looking for ways of decreasing outflows, limit fuel utilization, and take on eco-accommodating practices.

This obligation to supportability isn't just determined by administrative prerequisites yet in addition mirrors a more extensive industry acknowledgment of the significance of dependable sea rehearses.

The Maersk Triple-E class compartment ships, prestigious for their size and proficiency, are likewise prominent for their obligation to natural maintainability. These vessels consolidate cutting edge innovations, for example, squander heat recuperation frameworks, advanced structure plans, and energy-proficient motors. The execution of these elements lines up with the business' objectives to diminish ozone harming substance discharges and limit the environmental impression of sea transportation.

In seaward wind energy, oceanic innovation assumes a urgent part in the development and support of wind ranches. Particular vessels outfitted with dynamic situating frameworks and weighty lift capacities transport and introduce gigantic breeze turbine parts in remote ocean conditions. The combination of environmentally friendly power into sea tasks mirrors a more extensive industry pattern towards cleaner and more feasible practices.

The difficulties of present day oceanic innovation stretch out past development to the upkeep and decommissioning of vessels. In the seaward business, where designs are presented to unforgiving ecological circumstances, occasional assessments and upkeep are urgent to guaranteeing the trustworthiness of establishments. The Spearheading Soul, with its extraordinary twin-hulled plan and lifting limit, addresses a pivotal way to deal with decommissioning seaward stages in a solitary piece, limiting the natural effect of such exercises.

As vessels become bigger and more complicated, wellbeing stays a principal worry in present day sea innovation. High level security highlights, including modern route frameworks, crash aversion innovations, and crisis reaction conventions, are coordinated into the plan and activity of goliath ships. Besides, progressing innovative work endeavors center around improving wellbeing through developments, for example, independent vessels and high level life-saving advancements.

The investigation of independent vessels epitomizes the outskirts of present day sea innovation. Automated surface vessels (USVs) and independent submerged vehicles (AUVs) are progressively being sent for undertakings, for example, oceanographic research, submerged studies, and even freight transport. The improvement of independent delivery addresses a change in outlook in the business, with likely ramifications for functional effectiveness, wellbeing, and team government assistance.

The development of present day oceanic innovation has changed the development of huge vessels as well as reclassified the functional scene of the delivery business. As we dig further into the complexities of contemporary oceanic innovation, we experience extra aspects that add to the effectiveness, security, and manageability of gigantic boats.

One basic part of present day sea innovation is the accentuation on energy proficiency and outflow decrease. As the oceanic business faces expanding strain to moderate its ecological effect, vessel administrators are putting resources into imaginative answers for limit fuel utilization and discharges. High level impetus frameworks, like melted flammable gas (LNG) motors and crossover electric frameworks, are turning out to be more predominant, offering a cleaner and more supportable option in contrast to customary diesel motors.

The LNG-controlled vessels address an essential improvement chasing harmless to the ecosystem oceanic arrangements. LNG is a cleaner-consuming fuel that fundamentally lessens sulfur and nitrogen oxide discharges, adding to further developed air quality and meeting severe natural guidelines. The reception of LNG drive frameworks mirrors the business' obligation to lessening its carbon impression and lining up with global endeavors to battle environmental change.

Notwithstanding elective energizes, the oceanic business is investigating the coordination of environmentally friendly power sources into vessel tasks. Sunlight based chargers, wind turbines, and other environmentally friendly power advances are being integrated into transport plans to bridle normal assets and lessen dependence on conventional petroleum derivatives. The investigation of wind-helped drive situation, for example, inflexible sails and Flettner rotors, exhibits a pledge to bridling the force of nature to productively impel ships.

The reconciliation of computerized innovations and information examination is one more groundbreaking part of present day sea innovation. The idea of the "shrewd boat" use availability, sensors, and continuous information investigation to advance vessel execution, upgrade wellbeing, and smooth out functional cycles. Prescient support calculations, condition-based checking, and execution advancement apparatuses empower transport administrators to proactively oversee upkeep plans, decreasing free time and limiting the gamble of gear disappointments.

The Maersk Triple-E class compartment ships represent the marriage of advanced innovations and sea activities. These vessels use progressed information investigation to screen different parts of their exhibition, from motor productivity to freight conditions. The continuous experiences acquired from these advancements engage administrators to settle on informed choices, further develop eco-friendliness, and upgrade generally speaking functional adequacy.

Besides, the coming of independent delivery addresses a change in perspective in sea innovation. Automated surface vessels (USVs) and independent submerged vehicles (AUVs) are at the very front of this change, with the possibility to upset different parts of sea tasks. The advancement of independent vessels is driven by the possibility of expanded effectiveness, diminished functional expenses, and further developed security through the disposal of human mistake.

Independent advancements are especially encouraging in situations where normal and dreary errands can be proficiently dealt with by machines. In the transportation business, independent vessels can possibly improve course arranging, upgrade impact evasion, and smooth out route processes. The continuous examination and testing of independent boats mark an intense move toward a future where automated vessels coincide with customary monitored armadas, offering a brief look into the following boondocks of sea innovation.

As we investigate the diverse idea of current oceanic innovation, it becomes clear that the development of huge vessels is certainly not a detached accomplishment yet an interconnected undertaking that incorporates the whole lifecycle of a boat. From the plan and development stage, where best in class materials and impetus frameworks are coordinated, to the functional stage, where digitalization and independent innovations upgrade effectiveness, the oceanic business is developing into a dynamic and mechanically refined space.

The mission for developing and working monster ships fit for exploring profound seas is a continuous excursion set apart by consistent advancement and variation to arising difficulties. The crossing point of designing brightness, manageability goals, and computerized progressions impels the sea business toward a future where vessels vanquish the profundities as well as do as such with uplifted proficiency, decreased natural effect, and an unfaltering obligation to somewhere safe in the tremendous scope of the world's seas.

4.2 Discussion of submersibles, submarines, and other cutting-edge technologies in the realm of underwater exploration.

The domain of submerged investigation has seen striking headways in state of the art advances, going from subs to submarines, pushing the limits of human comprehension and uncovering the secrets covered underneath the sea's surface. This conversation digs into the complexities of these creative advancements, investigating their verifiable turn of events, contemporary applications, and their part in extending our insight into the submerged world.

Submarines, particular watercraft intended for submerged investigation, play had a crucial impact in propelling comprehension we might interpret the remote ocean. From early subs like the Bathyscaphe Trieste to cutting edge research vessels, these vehicles have empowered researchers and pioneers to dive to extraordinary profundities, leading exploration, catching symbolism, and making momentous disclosures.

The Bathyscaphe Trieste, planned by Swiss designer Auguste Piccard, impacted the world forever in 1960 when it plunged to the Challenger Profound, the most profound point on the planet's seas. Steered by Jacques Piccard and Wear Walsh, the Trieste arrived at a profundity of around 35,797 feet (10,911 meters), giving mankind's most memorable direct perceptions of the secretive deep profundities. This famous sub displayed the potential for investigating outrageous conditions and prepared for resulting developments in submerged investigation.

In the contemporary time, subs have developed into complex exploration vessels outfitted with cutting edge innovations for logical examinations. The Alvin sub, worked by the Forest Opening Oceanographic Organization, has been instrumental in investigating aqueous vents, remote ocean environments, and the destruction of the Titanic. Alvin's minimized plan permits it to arrive at profundities of up to 14,764 feet (4,500 meters), giving scientists a flexible instrument for concentrating on many submerged peculiarities.

Another prominent submarine is the remotely worked vehicle (ROV) Jason, frequently utilized related to Alvin for extensive remote ocean investigation. Jason is associated with the surface vessel by a link and is outfitted with superior quality cameras, controller arms, and concentrated sensors. This couple approach of using both monitored and automated submarines permits analysts to direct complex investigations, gather tests, and catch nitty gritty symbolism of the sea depths.

Submarines, while essentially connected with military applications, have likewise assumed a critical part in logical examination and submerged investigation. Atomic fueled submarines, for example, those utilized by naval forces all over the planet, have the capacity to work lowered for broadened periods, giving a stage to logical missions, oceanographic examination, and planning the sea depths.

Lately, confidential undertakings and associations committed to sea investigation have entered the scene, adding to the improvement of state of the art submarines. OceanGate's Titan sub, for instance, addresses another age of monitored subs intended for remote ocean investigation. With a profundity rating of 4,000 meters, Titan is equipped for arriving at huge profundities, opening up potential open doors for business adventures, research drives, and submerged paleohistory.

Past customary submarines, independent submerged vehicles (AUVs) have become basic to submerged investigation. AUVs are untethered vehicles that work independently, following pre-modified ways or adjusting to constant information. These vehicles are furnished with sensors, cameras, and logical instruments, permitting them to catch point by point information on the sea climate.

The utilization of AUVs has reformed marine examination, empowering researchers to direct enormous scope overviews, map tremendous breadths of the sea depths, and study marine life in their regular territories. The REMUS (Far off Ecological Observing UnitS) series of AUVs, created by the Forest Opening Oceanographic Establishment, embodies the adaptability and viability of independent submerged vehicles in logical exploration.

One of the weighty parts of submerged investigation is the revelation and investigation of aqueous vents. These remote ocean biological systems, found along mid-sea edges, have a one of a kind exhibit of living things adjusted to outrageous circumstances. Submarines and AUVs furnished with particular instruments have been pivotal in uncovering the secrets of these conditions, uncovering the presence of already obscure species and environments.

State of the art advances in submerged investigation reach out to the field of marine paleontology, where submarines and remotely worked vehicles add to the revelation and protection of lowered social legacy. The investigation of old wrecks, for example, the Antikythera wreck off the shoreline of Greece, has given important experiences into authentic oceanic shipping lanes, shipbuilding methods, and social collaborations.

Headways in submerged advanced mechanics have additionally led to the improvement of delicate advanced mechanics, enlivened by the adaptability and versatility of marine creatures. Delicate automated frameworks, intended to mirror the developments of submerged animals, hold guarantee for fragile activities in conditions where unbending designs might be illogical. These delicate mechanical advances have likely applications in submerged investigation, sea life science, and natural observing.

The investigation of outrageous submerged conditions, like the Icy and Antarctic locales, requires particular advancements equipped for enduring cruel circumstances. Icebreaking submarines, outfitted with built up structures and strong impetus frameworks, explore through polar ice to lead research, concentrate on marine life, and add to how we might interpret the effect of environmental change on polar districts.

The intermingling of man-made reasoning (artificial intelligence) and submerged investigation has opened new roads for information examination and navigation. Simulated intelligence calculations are utilized to deal with enormous datasets gathered from subs, AUVs, and other submerged vehicles, separating significant experiences and recognizing designs in the huge and complex submerged climate. These man-made intelligence driven investigations upgrade the effectiveness of exploration endeavors and add to a more profound comprehension of marine biological systems.

In the domain of submerged investigation, the advancement of cross breed advancements, consolidating parts of subs and independent frameworks, is not too far off.

Crossover vehicles, like the HUGIN Half breed AUV/ROV created by Kongsberg Oceanic, flawlessly change among independent and remotely worked modes, offering adaptability in investigation missions. These crossover approaches augment the upsides of both independent and monitored frameworks, giving scientists adaptable instruments for submerged examinations.

The difficulties of investigating the remote ocean reach out past mechanical contemplations to incorporate moral contemplations, protection endeavors, and global joint effort. The fragile harmony between logical interest and natural effect highlights the significance of dependable investigation rehearses. Drives, for example, the "Blue Corona" project, zeroed in on the protection of marine assets, embody the obligation to supportable submerged investigation and the conservation of delicate biological systems.

Proceeding with our investigation of subs, submarines, and state of the art advancements in the domain of submerged investigation, it is basic to dive into the particular applications and accomplishments that have denoted the advancement of these trend setting innovations. From the most profound channels to polar ice-shrouded oceans, these vehicles play had a significant impact in extending how we might interpret the seas and their occupants.

One of the prominent accomplishments in the field of submarines is the investigation of the Mariana Channel. This channel, home to the Challenger Profound, the most profound point on The planet, has been a point of convergence for submerged investigation. The improvement of submarines equipped for enduring the outrageous tensions of the channel has empowered researchers to lead remarkable examinations in this difficult climate.

James Cameron's Deepsea Challenger, a submarine intended for solo jumps, dropped into the Challenger Somewhere down in 2012. This memorable excursion, arriving at profundities of more than 35,000 feet (10,994 meters), denoted a huge achievement in the investigation of the Mariana Channel. The information and tests gathered during this campaign add to how we might interpret the geography, science, and hydrodynamics of perhaps of the least-investigated district in the world.

In the domain of sea life science, subs and remotely worked vehicles (ROVs) have been instrumental in concentrating on remote ocean biological systems and marine life. The revelation of aqueous vents, overflowing with remarkable and frequently extremophilic living beings, has reshaped how we might interpret life's flexibility to outrageous circumstances. Subs like Alvin and ROVs like Jason have permitted researchers to notice, gather tests, and archive the way of behaving of species right at home.

The Monterey Narrows Aquarium Exploration Foundation's (MBARI) utilization of the remotely worked vehicle Doc Ricketts represents the commitments of ROVs to sea life science.

Doc Ricketts has investigated the profundities of the Pacific Sea, giving researchers high-goal symbolism and the capacity to gather examples from already difficult to reach profundities. The revelations made by these high level vehicles have divulged new species and tested predispositions about the constraints of life in the remote ocean.

Submarines, while generally connected with military applications, have likewise assumed a vital part in logical undertakings. The investigation of polar districts, where ice-covered oceans present special difficulties, has profited from the capacities of submarines intended for icebreaking. These submarines explore through thick ice to arrive at distant areas, leading exploration on environmental change, oceanography, and the elements of polar biological systems.

The Siberian Government College's exploration submarine Mir-1 and Mir-2 have been conveyed in the Cold Sea to concentrate on the seabed and lead research in the difficult Icy climate. These submarines, fit for getting through ice, empower researchers to investigate locales that sounds blocked off, truly. The information gathered from these missions add to how we might interpret the effects of environmental change in the Icy and the extraordinary biological systems that flourish in outrageous circumstances.

Headways in submerged mechanical technology have extended the extent of investigation, especially in the area of prehistoric studies. Submarines furnished with cutting edge imaging situation and controller arms permit archeologists to investigate and report lowered archeological locales, opening the mysteries of antiquated human advancements. Remarkable disclosures incorporate antiquated wrecks, lowered urban areas, and ancient rarities that give bits of knowledge into authentic shipping lanes and sea societies.

The utilization of remotely worked vehicles, for example, the Hercules ROV worked by the Sea Investigation Trust, has worked with archeological examinations in remote ocean conditions. The investigation of the Antikythera wreck, a prominent archeological site off the shore of Greece, involved the utilization of cutting edge ROV innovation to recuperate curios and make nitty gritty guides of the submerged site. These archeological undertakings add to the conservation of social legacy and the disentangling of oceanic history.

Chasing after ecological protection and economical practices, submerged investigation advances have been conveyed to study and screen marine environments. Independent submerged vehicles (AUVs) furnished with sensors for water quality investigation, natural surroundings planning, and biodiversity evaluations contribute important information for marine protection endeavors. These advances help in the recognizable proof of safeguarded regions, observing of jeopardized species, and evaluation of the effect of human exercises on marine conditions.

The reconciliation of computerized reasoning (man-made intelligence) into submerged investigation innovations has additionally upgraded their capacities. Simulated intelligence calculations investigate immense datasets gathered from subs, AUVs, and different sources, distinguishing examples, oddities, and likely areas of premium. This information driven approach works on the effectiveness of submerged investigation by smoothing out the recognizable proof of experimentally huge highlights and upgrading research endeavors.

The continuous investigation of the seas includes cooperative endeavors on a global scale. The sharing of advancements, research discoveries, and assets is vital for propelling comprehension we might interpret the worldwide sea framework. Drives, for example, the Nippon Establishment GEBCO Seabed 2030 venture intend to plan the whole ocean bottom continuously 2030, cultivating global cooperation and utilizing the abilities of cutting edge subs and AUVs to accomplish this aggressive objective.

With regards to remote ocean mining, where the extraction of minerals from the sea depths presents both monetary open doors and natural difficulties, submerged investigation innovations assume a urgent part. Submarines outfitted with inspecting instruments and remotely worked vehicles are conveyed to survey mineral stores, concentrate on remote ocean biological systems, and assess the possible effects of mining exercises. These advancements add to educated navigation and the improvement regarding capable practices in the arising field of remote ocean mining.

Planning ahead, the development of submerged investigation advances is ready to address arising difficulties and open doors. The advancement of half and half vehicles that flawlessly change among independent and monitored modes, the coordination of delicate mechanical technology for sensitive tasks, and the proceeded with refinement of man-made intelligence driven information investigation are among the patterns molding the following period of submerged investigation.

The conversation of subs, submarines, and state of the art advancements in submerged investigation features the surprising accomplishments and progressing headways that have pushed mankind into the profundities of the seas. From the Mariana Channel to polar ice-shrouded oceans, from sea life science to paleontology and ecological protection, these advances have become key devices for disentangling the secrets of the submerged world. As we explore the unknown domains underneath the surface, the cooperative energy of advancement, joint effort, and moral stewardship stays fundamental for the proceeded with investigation and comprehension of Earth's last wilderness.

Chapter 5

Environmental Challenges and Solutions

Ecological difficulties in the 21st century have arrived at a basic crossroads, requiring pressing consideration, creative arrangements, and worldwide participation. From environmental change and biodiversity misfortune to contamination and asset exhaustion, the effects of human exercises in the world are significant and expansive. This conversation investigates the complex natural difficulties looked by mankind and digs into the different cluster of arrangements and methodologies that are fundamental for encouraging a practical and tough future.

At the front of natural worries is environmental change, driven basically by the aggregation of ozone harming substances in the World's air. The consuming of petroleum derivatives, deforestation, and modern exercises have essentially expanded centralizations of carbon dioxide (CO_2), methane (CH_4), and other ozone depleting substances. The outcomes of environmental change incorporate climbing worldwide temperatures, more continuous and serious outrageous climate occasions, disturbances to biological systems, and dangers to food and water security.

Relieving environmental change requires an extensive and coordinated approach that tends to both the circumstances and end results of this worldwide peculiarity. Progressing to sustainable power sources, for example, sunlight based, wind, and hydropower, is a vital stage in diminishing dependence on petroleum products. Putting resources into energy-effective advances, taking on feasible practices in farming, and advancing afforestation and reforestation endeavors add to bringing down ozone harming substance outflows and upgrading the planet's ability to assimilate carbon.

Notwithstanding environmental change, biodiversity misfortune represents a critical test to the wellbeing and versatility of biological systems around the world. Human exercises, including natural surroundings obliteration, overexploitation of species, contamination, and the presentation of obtrusive species, have prompted a quick decrease in biodiversity. This deficiency of species variety reduces the inherent worth of biological systems as well as subverts their capacity to offer fundamental types of assistance, like fertilization, water cleansing, and illness guideline.

Moderating biodiversity requires the insurance of normal living spaces, the foundation of safeguarded regions, and the execution of supportable land-use rehearses. Endeavors to battle unlawful natural life exchange and poaching are vital for protecting jeopardized species. Besides, supporting local area based preservation drives and coordinating biodiversity contemplations into improvement arranging are fundamental parts of a thorough technique to resolve the complicated issue of biodiversity misfortune.

The unavoidable test of contamination further mixtures natural corruption, influencing air, water, and soil quality. Air contamination, driven by modern emanations, vehicle exhaust, and the consuming of petroleum products, presents critical dangers to human wellbeing and compounds respiratory and cardiovascular infections. Essentially, water contamination, coming about because of modern releases, horticultural overflow, and inappropriate garbage removal, undermines oceanic biological systems and risks admittance to clean water for human populaces.

Tending to contamination requires rigid administrative measures, the implementation of natural regulations, and the advancement of cleaner innovations and practices across businesses. Putting resources into wastewater treatment offices, executing waste decrease and reusing projects, and raising public mindfulness about the effects of contamination are basic parts of an all encompassing way to deal with moderating natural contamination.

Asset exhaustion, driven by unreasonable utilization designs and over-extraction of regular assets, is another basic natural test. The exhaustion of limited assets, like freshwater, minerals, and arable land, presents dangers to both environmental honesty and human prosperity. Unreasonable fishing practices, deforestation, and the consumption of springs add to the debasement of biological systems and compromise the accessibility of fundamental assets.

Practical asset the board includes embracing roundabout economy standards, limiting waste, and advancing mindful utilization. Protection rehearses in agribusiness, for example, agroecology and accuracy cultivating, assist with enhancing asset use while keeping up with soil wellbeing and biodiversity. Carrying out water preservation measures, safeguarding basic environments, and cultivating global participation on asset the executives are fundamental for tending to the intricate snare of difficulties related with asset exhaustion.

The interconnection of these natural difficulties highlights the requirement for a comprehensive and foundational way to deal with manageability. Perceiving the multifaceted connections between environmental change, biodiversity misfortune, contamination, and asset exhaustion is fundamental for planning viable and incorporated arrangements. A progress to a more reasonable and regenerative model of improvement is basic for moderating ecological difficulties and protecting an amicable concurrence with the planet.

Environmentally friendly power arises as a key part in the change to a low-carbon and maintainable energy future. Saddling the force of sun powered, wind, hydropower, and geothermal energy offers a feasible option in contrast to petroleum derivatives, diminishing ozone depleting substance outflows and moderating the effects of environmental change. Interest in environmentally friendly power foundation, innovative work, and strategy systems that boost the reception of clean energy innovations are essential parts of a maintainable energy progress.

Moreover, energy productivity estimates assume a vital part in diminishing by and large energy utilization and improving the viability of environmentally friendly power arrangements. The execution of energy-proficient advances in structures, transportation, and modern cycles adds to bringing down carbon impressions and improving asset use. Drives advancing energy protection, for example, retrofitting structures for further developed protection and effectiveness, show substantial advancement in moderating natural effects.

In the horticultural area, economical practices are instrumental in addressing natural difficulties connected with biodiversity misfortune, contamination, and asset exhaustion. Agroecological approaches, which underscore the incorporation of environmental standards into horticultural frameworks, advance soil wellbeing, decrease dependence on compound information sources, and upgrade biodiversity on farmlands. Accuracy cultivating advances, including information driven direction and accuracy water system, streamline asset use and limit ecological effects.

Reconsidering utilization examples and embracing roundabout economy standards address groundbreaking answers for the test of asset exhaustion. The roundabout economy focuses on the decrease, reuse, and reusing of materials, intending to limit squander and expand the life expectancy of items. Developments in item plan that focus on sturdiness, reparability, and recyclability add to a more supportable way to deal with asset use.

In the domain of biodiversity preservation, the foundation and successful administration of safeguarded regions are basic for protecting environments and defending weak species. Safeguarded regions act as shelters for biodiversity, permitting biological systems to recuperate and giving fundamental territories to imperiled species. Local area based preservation drives, including nearby networks in the stewardship of regular assets, improve the viability and manageability of safeguarded regions.

Besides, coordinating biodiversity contemplations into land-use arranging and improvement processes forestalls natural surroundings obliteration and fracture. Rebuilding endeavors, including reforestation undertakings and natural surroundings restoration, add to the recuperation of environments and backing biodiversity preservation. Cooperative drives between state run administrations, non-legislative associations, and nearby networks are fundamental for accomplishing significant and enduring results in biodiversity preservation.

The test of contamination requests a complete and cooperative reaction to address both the sources and outcomes of ecological defilement. Tough guidelines and authorization instruments are fundamental for controling modern emanations, managing garbage removal, and moderating air and water contamination. Worldwide collaboration is essential for tending to transboundary contamination and guaranteeing that countries cooperate to battle shared ecological difficulties.

With regards to air contamination, progressing to cleaner and sustainable power hotspots for transportation and modern cycles fundamentally lessens outflows of poisons like nitrogen oxides and particulate matter. In metropolitan regions, the advancement of public transportation, cycling foundation, and green spaces adds to further developed air quality and the prosperity of metropolitan populaces. Furthermore, progressions in innovation, for example, electric vehicles and emanation control frameworks, assume a critical part in relieving the effects of air contamination.

Wastewater the board and the treatment of modern effluents are vital to tending to water contamination. Carrying out cutting edge wastewater treatment innovations, upholding profluent guidelines, and advancing the protected removal of dangerous waste add to keeping up with water quality. Rebuilding endeavors, for example, the restoration of dirtied water bodies and the expulsion of impurities, are fundamental for reestablishing environments and guaranteeing the accessibility of clean water for networks.

Public mindfulness and training efforts assume a crucial part in cultivating a feeling of obligation and empowering supportable ways of behaving. Enabling people and networks with information about the results of contamination, the significance of waste decrease, and the advantages of maintainable living adds to an aggregate work to battle natural debasement.

Instructive drives, especially in schools and nearby networks, develop a feeling of natural stewardship and motivate people in the future to focus on supportability.

Asset exhaustion, especially with regards to fisheries and water assets, requires the execution of feasible administration rehearses. Embracing science-based fisheries the executives systems, for example, get cutoff points and environment security, forestalls overfishing and advances the recuperation of fish stocks. Reasonable water the executives works on, including watershed insurance, productive water system strategies, and the reclamation of corrupted environments, add to the conservation of freshwater assets.

Worldwide coordinated effort is essential for tending to worldwide difficulties related with asset exhaustion, as numerous normal assets cross public lines. Arrangements and structures that advance dependable asset extraction, fair sharing of advantages, and the counteraction of unlawful and unreasonable practices add to a more economical and versatile worldwide asset framework.

The interconnected idea of natural difficulties features the significance of embracing an all encompassing and frameworks situated way to deal with supportability. Cross-sectoral coordinated effort, informed independent direction, and the combination of ecological contemplations into strategies and practices are fundamental for tending to the mind boggling trap of difficulties confronting the planet. The accomplishment of the Practical Improvement Objectives (SDGs), especially Objective 13 on environment activity, Objective 14 on life underneath water, and Objective 15 on life ashore, highlights the worldwide obligation to ecological supportability.

The job of innovation and advancement in tending to ecological difficulties couldn't possibly be more significant. Leap forwards in clean energy advancements, supportable farming practices, and contamination control measures add to the change towards an additional maintainable and strong future. Innovative work drives zeroed in on ecological advancement encourage the rise of state of the art arrangements that can possibly change ventures and alleviate natural effects.

Mechanical developments in squander the executives, like the improvement of cutting edge reusing advancements and waste-to-energy frameworks, add to limiting the natural impression of human exercises. Shrewd innovations, including sensor organizations and information investigation, upgrade natural observing and empower more powerful reactions to contamination occurrences. The coordination of advanced advances into ecological administration frameworks gives ongoing information, works with informed navigation, and advances straightforwardness in tending to natural difficulties.

The roundabout economy, with its accentuation on shutting the circle of material streams, presents a change in perspective in how social orders approach asset use and waste age.

Round plans of action, like item as-a-administration and sharing economy stages, advance asset effectiveness and diminish the ecological effect of utilization. Advancements in materials science, including the improvement of biodegradable and economical materials, add to diminishing the biological impression of businesses and items.

Green money and reasonable venture assume a urgent part in driving the change to an all the more harmless to the ecosystem and socially mindful economy. Monetary foundations, organizations, and financial backers are progressively perceiving the significance of integrating ecological, social, and administration (ESG) standards into dynamic cycles. Supportable money drives, green securities, and effect effective money management channels capital towards undertakings and adventures that focus on natural supportability and add to positive social results.

The job of strategy and administration in tending to ecological difficulties couldn't possibly be more significant. Strong ecological strategies, upheld by successful requirement components, are fundamental for controlling modern exercises, safeguarding regular natural surroundings, and moderating the effects of environmental change. Peaceful accords, for example, the Paris Settlement on environmental change and the Show on Natural Variety, give systems to worldwide joint effort and obligation to tending to shared ecological difficulties.

Public and neighborhood states assume a focal part in molding strategies that advance maintainability, versatility, and ecological stewardship. Regulation that boosts environmentally friendly power reception, directs emanations, and empowers supportable land-use rehearses adds to establishing an empowering climate for ecological protection. The combination of ecological contemplations into metropolitan preparation, framework advancement, and fiasco risk decrease endeavors upgrades the supportability of human settlements.

Cooperation between states, organizations, common society, and the scholarly community is pivotal for executing far reaching answers for ecological difficulties. Multi-stakeholder organizations and drives work with the sharing of information, assets, and mastery, encouraging an aggregate way to deal with resolving mind boggling and interconnected natural issues. The commitment of assorted partners guarantees that arrangements are setting explicit, comprehensive, and receptive to the requirements of networks and biological systems.

Natural training and public mindfulness crusades are necessary parts of encouraging a culture of supportability. Engaging people with information about the climate, manageable practices, and the outcomes of human exercises in the world develops a feeling of obligation and empowers informed navigation. Instructive drives at schools, colleges, and local area associations add to building an age of naturally cognizant residents who effectively take part in the change to a maintainable future.

The natural difficulties confronting mankind request a deliberate and ground-breaking work to defend the planet for current and people in the future. The interconnected idea of environmental change, biodiversity misfortune, contamination, and asset consumption requires coordinated arrangements that address the underlying drivers of natural debasement. A change in perspective towards maintainability, driven by mechanical development, strategy soundness, and aggregate activity, is fundamental for making a tough and agreeable connection among mankind and the planet. The quest for ecological supportability isn't just an ethical basic however a functional need for guaranteeing the prosperity of the Earth and its occupants in the long stretches of time to come.

5.1 Examination of the environmental impact of large ships.

The natural effect of enormous boats is an intricate and diverse issue that traverses across different aspects, incorporating air and water contamination, ozone harming substance discharges, and environmental unsettling influences. As basic parts of worldwide exchange and transportation organizations, huge boats assume a vital part in working with the development of products across seas. Notwithstanding, their natural impression raises worries about the manageability of sea exercises and prompts the investigation of inventive answers for moderate antagonistic impacts.

One huge part of the natural effect of enormous boats is air contamination. The ignition of non-renewable energy sources in transport motors discharges poisons like sulfur dioxide (SO2), nitrogen oxides (NOx), particulate matter (PM), and carbon dioxide (CO2) into the climate. Conventional marine powers, especially weighty fuel oil, have high sulfur content, prompting raised SO2 emanations and adding to air quality debasement, especially in waterfront regions and port urban areas.

The Global Sea Association (IMO), perceiving the ecological results of air contamination from transportation, has acquainted guidelines with address this issue. The

Global Show for the Anticipation of Contamination from Boats (MARPOL) Addition VI draws certain lines on the sulfur content of marine fills and lays out rules for the decrease of NOx discharges. The reception of low-sulfur powers and the execution of fumes gas cleaning frameworks, known as scrubbers, address estimates utilized by the transportation business to follow these guidelines and relieve air contamination.

Notwithstanding ordinary air contaminations, the sea area is a huge supporter of worldwide ozone harming substance emanations. CO2, a significant ozone harming substance, is delivered during the burning of petroleum products in transport motors. The long home season of CO2 in the air adds to environmental change, prompting rising ocean levels, modified atmospheric conditions, and disturbances to biological systems. Endeavors to address this challenge incorporate the turn of events and reception of elective powers, like condensed flammable gas (LNG) and biofuels, which have lower fossil fuel byproducts contrasted with conventional marine energizes.

Besides, the idea of "slow steaming" has gotten momentum as a system to decrease fuel utilization and lower CO2 outflows. This approach includes working boats at lower speeds, advancing journey arranging, and further developing eco-friendliness. While slow steaming presents financial and natural advantages, it likewise brings up issues about the harmony among supportability and the opportune conveyance of merchandise in a globalized economy.

Weight water the board is one more ecological concern related with huge boats. Counterbalance water, accepted for solidness and equilibrium, frequently contains a different cluster of oceanic species. At the point when released in various areas, these non-local species can upset nearby biological systems, outcompeting local species, spreading sicknesses, and causing natural irregular characteristics. To resolve this issue, the IMO's Counterweight Water The board Show sets guidelines for the treatment and release of counterbalance water to limit the exchange of obtrusive species.

The issue of submerged commotion contamination produced by enormous boats has likewise arisen as a subject of ecological concern. Transport produced clamor, basically from motor and propeller vibrations, can negatively affect marine life, especially marine vertebrates that depend on sound for correspondence, route, and taking care of. The steady foundation commotion from transportation traffic can slow down the normal ways of behaving of marine species, prompting pressure, bewilderment, and, at times, strandings.

Endeavors to alleviate submerged clamor contamination include the turn of events and reception of calmer boat plans, elective drive frameworks, and the execution of speed and course the executives measures to decrease in general commotion levels. Moreover, examination into the likely effects of submerged commotion on marine biological systems and the foundation of clamor confined zones plan to safeguard weak species and protect the acoustic honesty of sea conditions.

The issue of boat produced squander, including plastics, sewage, and perilous materials, adds one more layer to the ecological effect of enormous boats. Ill-advised removal rehearses and lacking waste administration frameworks on boats can bring about the arrival of contaminations into the marine climate. The release of untreated sewage presents endangers to water quality and marine life, while the presence of plastic garbage adds to the unavoidable issue of marine plastic contamination.

Guidelines, like MARPOL Addition V, lay out rules for the counteraction of contamination by trash from ships and preclude the removal of plastics adrift. The compelling execution of waste administration rehearses on ships, including the partition, stockpiling, and removal of various sorts of waste, is fundamental for limiting the natural effect of boat produced squander. Also, public mindfulness missions and industry drives add to advancing capable garbage removal rehearses among transport administrators and team individuals.

The ecological effect of huge boats reaches out past quick contaminations to the more extensive issue of the carbon impression related with transport development and activity. The creation and upkeep of enormous boats include energy-escalated processes, from the extraction and handling of natural substances to the assembling of boat parts and the development of vessels. The fossil fuel byproducts related with shipbuilding, known as "inserted outflows," add to the generally speaking natural effect of the sea business.

Endeavors to address the carbon impression of huge boats remember advancements for transport plan and development strategies to improve energy productivity. The utilization of lightweight materials, for example, high level composites and aluminum amalgams, diminishes the general load of vessels, prompting fuel investment funds and lower discharges during activity. Moreover, the investigation of elective impetus innovations, for example, wind-helped drive frameworks and half and half electric frameworks, plans to additionally lessen the natural effect of enormous boats.

The idea of "green delivery" envelops an all encompassing way to deal with supportability in the oceanic business. Green delivery drives center around incorporating harmless to the ecosystem practices and advancements into different parts of the transportation interaction, including vessel plan, impetus frameworks, fuel decisions, and functional practices. Industry partners, including shipowners, administrators, and grouping social orders, are progressively embracing green transportation practices to line up with ecological objectives and administrative prerequisites.

The rise of independent transportation addresses a mechanical headway with the possibility to impact the natural effect of huge boats. Automated surface vessels (USVs) and independent submerged vehicles (AUVs) are being investigated for different sea applications, including freight transport, reconnaissance, and information assortment. The reception of independent innovations can possibly upgrade course arranging, lessen fuel utilization, and improve generally functional proficiency, prompting a more practical and harmless to the ecosystem delivering industry.

Natural guidelines and peaceful accords assume a crucial part in forming the scene of reasonable delivery rehearses. The IMO, as the worldwide administrative body for the sea business, lays out norms and rules to address ecological difficulties and advance the reception of best practices. Administrative structures, for example, the Energy

Productivity Existing Boat Record (EEXI) and the Carbon Power Pointer (CII), plan to further develop the energy proficiency of existing boats and set focuses for the decrease of carbon power.

The worldwide push for decarbonization in different areas, including transporting, has prompted expanded examination of the oceanic business' job in adding to environmental change.

The Worldwide Sea Association's Underlying IMO System on Decrease of GHG Discharges from Boats frames a dream to diminish complete yearly ozone harming substance emanations from global transportation by something like half by 2050, contrasted with 2008 levels, and to seek after endeavors toward gradually eliminating outflows totally.

To accomplish these aggressive focuses on, the sea business is investigating a scope of elective powers and impetus innovations. Melted petroleum gas (LNG), hydrogen, alkali, and biofuels are among the choices being considered to supplant or supplement customary marine powers. The improvement of zero-outflow vessels, controlled by energy units or electric impetus, addresses a groundbreaking step towards decarbonizing the oceanic area.

The progress to elective powers faces difficulties connected with framework, accessibility, and cost-adequacy. Framework for bunkering elective energizes, for example, LNG or hydrogen, should be created at significant ports to help the reception of these cleaner energy sources. The expense seriousness of elective powers and the versatility of creation are significant variables that will impact the speed and degree of their incorporation into the transportation business.

The natural effect of huge boats is a diverse test that requires deliberate endeavors from the sea business, administrative bodies, and the worldwide local area. As a foundation of worldwide exchange, enormous boats should explore the fragile harmony between financial objectives and natural maintainability. The reception of cleaner advancements, adherence to rigid guidelines, and the quest for imaginative arrangements are fundamental for limiting the natural impression of enormous ships and guaranteeing a more maintainable future for the oceanic business. The continuous change to greener practices and the investigation of elective powers mark huge strides toward an all the more ecologically cognizant and dependable sea area.

5.2 Discussion of sustainable practices and technological innovations aimed at minimizing the ecological footprint of maritime giants.

The sea business, with its titanic vessels crossing the world's seas, assumes a crucial part in worldwide exchange and transportation. In any case, the natural effect of oceanic goliaths has provoked the investigation of economical practices and mechanical advancements to limit their biological impression. This conversation digs into the drives and progressions pointed toward encouraging an all the more earth cognizant and practical sea area.

One of the critical areas of concentration in moderating the environmental effect of oceanic goliaths is the reception of option and cleaner energizes. Conventional marine energizes, especially weighty fuel oil, add to air contamination through the emanation of sulfur dioxide (SO2), nitrogen oxides (NOx), and particulate matter. To address this, the business is progressively going to elective fills with lower outflows, like condensed gaseous petrol (LNG), hydrogen, and biofuels.

LNG, specifically, has built up forward momentum as a momentary fuel because of its lower sulfur content and decreased ozone harming substance emanations contrasted with customary marine energizes. LNG-fueled vessels have become more pervasive, with transport administrators putting resources into the important framework for melted flammable gas bunkering at significant ports. The utilization of LNG as a fuel addresses a huge step towards meeting natural guidelines, like the Global Sea Association's (IMO) sulfur cap, which restricts the sulfur content in marine energizes.

Hydrogen is arising as one more encouraging elective fuel for the sea business. Hydrogen energy components, which produce power through the response of hydrogen with oxygen, offer a zero-discharge drive arrangement. A few innovative work drives are in progress to investigate the practicality of hydrogen-controlled vessels, tending to both air quality and ozone harming substance outflow concerns. Notwithstanding, challenges connected with hydrogen creation, stockpiling, and framework should be tended to for far reaching reception.

Biofuels got from sustainable sources, like green growth or waste materials, present one more road for decreasing the carbon impression of oceanic goliaths. These reasonable powers offer a method for progressing away from non-renewable energy sources and add to the business' obligation to decarbonization. Progressing examination and pilot projects are investigating the practicality of biofuels as a versatile and harmless to the ecosystem answer for the sea area.

Notwithstanding elective energizes, headways in drive advances are reshaping the scene of practical transportation. Electric drive, either through battery frameworks or shore power associations, is acquiring unmistakable quality as a perfect and effective method for controlling vessels in port or for brief distance courses. Battery-electric and half and half electric impetus frameworks add to bring down outflows and further developed energy proficiency, especially during low-speed activities and while moving in restricted spaces.

Shore power, otherwise called cold pressing or option oceanic power (AMP), permits vessels to interface with the electrical matrix while berthed at a port. This wipes out the requirement for locally available generators, lessening discharges and commotion contamination in port regions. Ports overall are putting resources into shore power foundation to boost the reception of this reasonable practice by transport administrators.

Wind-helped drive addresses a centuries-old yet revived idea in maintainable transportation. The utilization of wind energy to enhance conventional drive frameworks has seen a resurgence with present day innovations, for example, rotor sails and kite sails. These frameworks outfit the force of the breeze to impel vessels, giving fuel reserve funds and emanations decrease. Wind-helped drive is especially viable during long journeys, and its joining into the plan of sea goliaths mirrors a promise to outfitting environmentally friendly power sources.

Advancements in frame plan and coatings add to the improvement of hydrodynamic effectiveness, diminishing drag and fuel utilization. Air oil frameworks, which discharge a floor covering of air pockets along the body to diminish contact with the water, have exhibited critical fuel reserve funds. Moreover, high level body coatings with low-grating properties and antifouling abilities forestall the collection of marine living beings on the boat's surface, further upgrading eco-friendliness.

Past drive and fuel contemplations, feasible practices in transport plan and development are essential for limiting the biological impression of oceanic goliaths. The idea of eco-accommodating boat configuration integrates standards, for example, lightweight materials, streamlined frame shapes, and energy-effective frameworks. Aluminum amalgams, composites, and other lightweight materials add to the development of vessels with diminished weight, upgrading eco-friendliness and by and large natural execution.

Transport reusing rehearses likewise assume a urgent part in the business' manageability endeavors. Mindful shipbreaking includes the safe and naturally sound destroying of resigned vessels, guaranteeing the legitimate removal of dangerous materials and the reusing of significant parts. Consistence with global guidelines, like the Hong Kong Worldwide Show for the Safe and Earth Sound Reusing of Boats, is fundamental for advancing manageable boat reusing rehearses and forestalling ecological damage.

The reception of computerized advances and information driven arrangements is altering the oceanic business, offering new roads for upgrading tasks and improving manageability. Shrewd delivery, empowered by the Web of Things (IoT) and high level sensor innovations, takes into consideration continuous observing and enhancement of vessel execution. Information examination give experiences into fuel utilization designs, motor proficiency, and journey arranging, empowering transport administrators to pursue informed choices that lessen ecological effect.

The execution of man-made brainpower (simulated intelligence) in oceanic tasks further improves proficiency and supportability. Man-made intelligence calculations can enhance course arranging, considering variables like weather patterns, ocean flows, and fuel utilization. Prescient support, empowered by simulated intelligence, limits personal time and diminishes the natural effect of upkeep related exercises. The joining of computerized twin advances takes into consideration programmatic experiences and demonstrating of vessel execution, working with consistent improvement and development.

The idea of independent transportation, frequently alluded to as automated surface vessels (USVs) or independent boats, addresses a groundbreaking jump in oceanic innovation. Independent vessels influence artificial intelligence, sensors, and navigational advancements to work without human mediation.

While the full-scale reception of independent transportation is still in its beginning phases, the potential advantages incorporate better wellbeing, improved functional productivity, and diminished ecological effect through advanced course arranging and energy-proficient tasks.

The manageable practices and mechanical developments examined are important for a more extensive all inclusive shift towards an all the more naturally cognizant and capable sea area. In any case, difficulties and obstructions endure, thwarting the broad reception of these drives. One huge test is the forthright expense related with the execution of green innovations and manageable practices. While the drawn out benefits as far as fuel reserve funds and natural stewardship are obvious, the underlying speculation can be an impediment for some boat administrators.

Framework limits additionally present difficulties for the reception of elective energizes and shore power. The accessibility of bunkering foundation for LNG, hydrogen, and biofuels isn't yet broad, restricting the courses and districts where vessels can progress to cleaner fills. Also, the extension of shore power framework requires critical ventures from both port specialists and boat administrators. Beating these foundation challenges is vital for understanding the maximum capacity of feasible sea rehearses.

The administrative scene assumes a significant part in forming the direction of maintainability in the sea business. While worldwide guidelines, for example, the IMO's MARPOL Addition VI, set emanation principles and rules for the utilization of elective energizes, the implementation and severity of these guidelines shift universally. A blended and reliably upheld administrative system is fundamental for guaranteeing a level battleground and empowering widespread reception of manageable practices.

Industry joint effort and information sharing stages are instrumental in conquering difficulties and driving reasonable advancement. Gatherings, organizations, and drives that unite shipowners, administrators, innovation suppliers, and administrative bodies encourage a cooperative way to deal with tending to normal difficulties. The sharing of best practices, examples learned, and innovative progressions speeds up the business' change towards manageability.

Public mindfulness and partner commitment are necessary parts of the business' maintainability process. Ecological stewardship and corporate social obligation have become central focuses for transport administrators looking to line up with cultural assumptions and add to worldwide endeavors to battle environmental change. Straightforward investigating ecological execution, emanations decreases, and maintainability drives improves responsibility and fabricates trust among partners.

5.3 Eco-friendly initiatives within the maritime industry.

The sea business, a foundation of worldwide exchange and transportation, is progressively embracing eco-accommodating drives to address natural worries and limit its biological impression. This shift towards supportability includes an expansive range of practices, innovations, and strategies pointed toward encouraging natural stewardship, decreasing emanations, and advancing mindful asset the executives inside the sea area. This conversation investigates a portion of the key eco-accommodating drives that are forming the fate of the sea business.

One principal part of the business' eco-accommodating drives spins around the reception of elective fills. Customary marine fills, described by high sulfur content and critical ozone harming substance discharges, have been a significant supporter of air contamination and environmental change. The change to cleaner and more manageable fills is vital for relieving these natural effects. Condensed Petroleum gas (LNG) has arisen as an unmistakable elective fuel, offering lower sulfur discharges and diminished carbon dioxide (CO2) emanations contrasted with customary marine fills. LNG-controlled vessels have become progressively predominant, and the improvement of LNG bunkering framework at significant ports upholds the business' obligation to this eco-accommodating fuel.

Hydrogen is one more elective fuel acquiring consideration inside the sea area. Hydrogen energy components, which produce power through the response of hydrogen with oxygen, offer a zero-emanation drive arrangement. While hydrogen-fueled vessels are still in the beginning phases of improvement and face difficulties connected with creation, stockpiling, and framework, they hold huge potential for accomplishing long haul supportability objectives. The investigation of hydrogen as an oceanic fuel lines up with more extensive endeavors to decarbonize the business and progress towards cleaner energy sources.

Biofuels got from inexhaustible sources have likewise arisen as a reasonable choice for lessening the carbon impression of oceanic tasks. Biofuels can be created from different feedstocks, including green growth, squander materials, and agrarian build-ups. These reasonable powers offer a pathway to diminish reliance on non-renewable energy sources and add to the business' obligation to harmless to the ecosystem rehearses. Progressing examination and pilot projects plan to survey the achievability and versatility of biofuels in the oceanic setting, preparing for their expanded reception.

Notwithstanding elective energizes, the business is seeing progressions in drive advancements that improve energy proficiency and lessen discharges. Electric impetus frameworks, controlled by batteries or shore associations, have acquired noticeable quality as perfect and productive answers for brief distance tasks and keeping in mind that vessels are berthed at ports.

Battery-electric and cross breed electric impetus frameworks add to bring down discharges, further developed mobility, and improved generally speaking functional effectiveness. The coordination of electric impetus lines up with the business' quest for eco-accommodating innovations that focus on maintainability and natural obligation.

Wind-helped drive addresses a centuries-old idea that is encountering a cutting edge resurgence as an eco-accommodating drive in the oceanic business. Advances, for example, rotor sails and kite sails bridle the force of the breeze to help with moving vessels, giving fuel reserve funds and diminishing discharges. Wind-helped drive frameworks are especially successful during long journeys and add to the business' endeavors to use environmentally friendly power sources. The coordination of wind-helped innovations into the plan and activity of vessels mirrors a guarantee to eco-accommodating practices that line up with more extensive supportability objectives.

Upgrades in frame plan and coatings are basic to the business' endeavors to improve hydrodynamic effectiveness and lessen fuel utilization. Air oil frameworks, which discharge a floor covering of air pockets along the body to lessen grating with the water, have exhibited critical fuel investment funds. Also, high level frame coatings with low-grinding properties and antifouling capacities forestall the gathering of marine creatures on the boat's surface, further upgrading eco-friendliness. These eco-accommodating advancements in structure configuration add to the business' obligation to decreasing its natural effect through superior functional productivity.

Eco-accommodating boat configuration envelops an all encompassing way to deal with maintainability, coordinating standards like lightweight materials, improved shapes, and energy-proficient frameworks. The utilization of lightweight materials, including aluminum combinations and high level composites, adds to the development of vessels with decreased weight, upgrading eco-friendliness and in general natural execution. Upgraded structure shapes and further developed optimal design further add to the decrease of drag, bringing down fuel utilization and outflows. Energy-effective frameworks, including progressed impetus innovations and installed energy the executives, are key parts of eco-accommodating boat plan that focus on manageability all through the vessel's lifecycle.

The idea of practical boat reusing has acquired conspicuousness as an eco-accommodating drive inside the sea business. Dependable shipbreaking includes the safe and earth sound destroying of resigned vessels, guaranteeing the legitimate removal of unsafe materials and the reusing of important parts. Consistence with worldwide guidelines, like the Hong Kong Global Show for the Safe and Ecologically Sound Reusing of Boats, is fundamental for advancing maintainable boat reusing rehearses and forestalling natural damage. The business' obligation to feasible boat reusing lines up with more extensive endeavors to limit the biological effect of sea activities and maintain mindful natural practices.

Digitalization and the reception of shrewd innovations are driving eco-accommodating drives inside the sea business. The Web of Things (IoT), high level sensors, and information examination empower ongoing checking and streamlining of vessel execution. Savvy transporting arrangements give experiences into fuel utilization designs, motor proficiency, and natural effect, enabling boat administrators to pursue informed choices that lessen emanations and work on generally speaking supportability. The mix of computerized reasoning (simulated intelligence) further improves proficiency and maintainability, with simulated intelligence calculations streamlining course arranging, foreseeing support needs, and working with information driven navigation.

The execution of independent transportation, described by automated surface vessels (USVs) or independent boats, addresses a groundbreaking eco-accommodating drive inside the oceanic area. Independent vessels influence simulated intelligence, sensors, and navigational innovations to work without human intercession. While the full-scale reception of independent transportation is as yet developing, the potential advantages incorporate superior wellbeing, improved functional productivity, and diminished ecological effect through upgraded course arranging and energy-proficient activities. Independent delivery lines up with the business' obligation to utilizing state of the art innovations for reasonable and eco-accommodating sea rehearses.

Shore power, otherwise called cold pressing or option sea power (AMP), is an eco-accommodating drive that permits vessels to interface with the electrical matrix while berthed at a port. This training takes out the requirement for locally available generators, lessening emanations and commotion contamination in port regions. Ports overall are putting resources into shore power framework to boost the reception of this feasible practice by transport administrators. Shore power lines up with the business' endeavors to decrease the natural effect of oceanic exercises, especially during times of vessel inertia at ports.

The eco-accommodating drives inside the oceanic business are not just determined by administrative consistence and natural obligation yet additionally by market interest and public discernment. Partners, including buyers, financial backers, and administrative bodies, progressively focus on supportability and anticipate that the oceanic business should exhibit a guarantee to eco-accommodating practices. Thus, shipowners and administrators are incorporating supportability contemplations into their business procedures, with an emphasis on decreasing emanations, taking on cleaner advancements, and embracing eco-accommodating developments.

Cooperative drives and industry organizations assume an essential part in progressing eco-accommodating practices inside the oceanic area. Gatherings, affiliations, and working gatherings unite partners from various sections of the business to share best practices, trade information, and team up on manageability drives.

These cooperative endeavors add to the turn of events and execution of eco-accommodating advances and practices that benefit the whole sea environment.

Public mindfulness and training likewise assume an essential part in advancing eco-accommodating drives inside the sea business. Natural stewardship and corporate social obligation have become essential parts of the business' story, with transport administrators effectively captivating in straightforward providing details regarding ecological execution and supportability drives. Instructive projects and effort endeavors add to building mindfulness among industry experts, policymakers, and the overall population about the significance of eco-accommodating practices in guaranteeing the drawn out soundness of the seas and the planet.

Chapter 6

Beyond Boundaries: Future Prospects

As the oceanic business explores through the powerful flows of innovative head-ways, ecological objectives, and worldwide difficulties, what's to come possibilities are molded by a dream that reaches out past conventional limits. The development of oceanic goliaths, moved by advancement and supportability, opens up new skylines that rethink the business' job in the worldwide scene. This investigation into what's in store possibilities of the oceanic area envelops a multi-layered venture, incorporating mechanical boondocks, natural stewardship, international movements, and the rethinking of worldwide exchange.

One of the characterizing elements of the oceanic business' future is the proceeded with combination of state of the art advancements that push vessels into the domain of brilliant transportation. The idea of independent vessels, driven by man-made reasoning (simulated intelligence), high level sensors, and AI, proclaims another time in oceanic activities.

Automated surface vessels (USVs) furnished with independent route frameworks guarantee expanded effectiveness, decreased functional expenses, and improved security. These vessels, fit for exploring huge sea fields without human mediation, address a change in perspective that rises above ordinary limits of sea tasks.

The ascent of independent delivery isn't simply an innovative wonder however an extraordinary power that rethinks the idea of sea work, wellbeing conventions, and functional elements. The sending of independent vessels presents novel contemplations regarding administrative structures, network safety, and the moral elements of man-made intelligence in dynamic cycles. While the combination of independent advancements guarantees proficiency gains and a decrease in human blunder, it likewise requires a powerful administrative system that guarantees wellbeing, security, and moral practices in sea tasks.

In equal, the appearance of advanced twins further enhances the business' capacities by making virtual reproductions of actual vessels, considering continuous checking, prescient upkeep, and execution improvement. Computerized twin innovations, driven by cutting edge information examination and recreation models, empower transport administrators to upgrade functional productivity, lessen personal time, and advance fuel utilization. This combination of digitalization, independence, and information driven independent direction rises above customary limits, preparing for a sea area that works at the front line of mechanical development.

The fate of sea exchange is complicatedly connected with the development of worldwide production network elements, shipping lanes, and international contemplations. As international movements reshape coalitions and exchange connections, sea courses are dependent upon recalibration. The Cold, when a frozen wilderness, is acquiring vital significance as liquefying ice opens up new delivery paths. The Northern Ocean Course, associating Asia and Europe through the Icy, presents the two valuable open doors and difficulties. While it offers a more limited course, diminishing travel times and fuel utilization, it likewise raises worries about natural effects, the absence of framework, and the requirement for specific vessels equipped for exploring cold waters.

Besides, the continuous improvement of the Belt and Street Drive (BRI) by China is reshaping sea exchange designs, making new passageways of availability that stretch across Asia, Europe, and Africa. The extension of port offices, framework projects, and financial coordinated efforts along the BRI courses imagines a complete organization that works with consistent sea exchange. In any case, the international ramifications of this drive, including worries about obligation maintainability and vital impact, present intricacies that reach out past the geological limits of sea courses.

In a future molded by mechanical development and international recalibrations, natural supportability arises as a focal topic that rises above industry limits. The basic to address environmental change, lessen outflows, and save marine biological systems is controlling the sea area towards a greener and more manageable future. The Worldwide Oceanic Association's (IMO) focuses for lessening ozone depleting substance (GHG) emanations from transportation signal an aggregate obligation to natural stewardship.

Elective fills, like condensed flammable gas (LNG), hydrogen, and biofuels, are at the front line of the oceanic business' mission for maintainability. The change towards cleaner energy sources lines up with administrative necessities as well as mirrors a proactive position towards lessening the business' carbon impression. LNG-controlled vessels, specifically, have acquired conspicuousness as an interval answer for satisfy discharge guidelines, offering lower sulfur content and diminished CO2 outflows contrasted with conventional marine powers. The investigation of hydrogen as an oceanic fuel, albeit in early stages, holds guarantee as a zero-outflow arrangement that rises above the limits of customary fuel sources.

Besides, the incorporation of sustainable power sources, like breeze and sun oriented power, into sea tasks imagines a future where vessels bridle the force of nature for drive and helper frameworks. Wind-helped drive frameworks, including rotor sails and kite sails, offer an economical method for lessening fuel utilization and outflows during journeys. The sending of sunlight based chargers on vessels adds to locally available power age, supporting assistant frameworks and diminishing dependence on customary power sources. These eco-accommodating drives not just rethink the limits of sea energy sources yet additionally highlight the business' obligation to a maintainable and mindful future.

As ecological contemplations become the overwhelming focus, the idea of round economy standards is building up forward movement inside the sea area. The round economy worldview tries to limit squander, advance reusing, and amplify asset proficiency. In transport plan and development, the joining of eco-accommodating materials, secluded parts, and recyclable materials lines up with the standards of a roundabout economy. Capable boat reusing works on, stressing the reuse of materials and legitimate removal of dangerous substances, epitomize a promise to supportable practices that reach out past the conventional limits of vessel lifecycle the executives.

The combination of maintainability and mechanical development reaches out to the domain of boat plan and development. Eco-accommodating boat plan standards focus on energy proficiency, decreased discharges, and the utilization of harmless to the ecosystem materials. Lightweight materials, for example, high level composites and aluminum compounds, add to the development of vessels with further developed eco-friendliness and diminished natural effect. Body plan developments, including air grease frameworks and high level coatings, upgrade hydrodynamic proficiency, further advancing fuel utilization. These headways reclassify the limits of what is conceivable in transport configuration, making vessels that embody an agreeable relationship with the climate.

Chasing supportability, the sea business is likewise embracing the idea of ecological, social, and administration (ESG) rules as a directing system for navigation. ESG contemplations reach out past the conventional monetary measurements, incorporating elements like ecological effect, social obligation, and corporate administration. Financial backers, partners, and customers are progressively focusing on organizations that show a pledge to ESG standards. This change in context rethinks the limits of progress for sea ventures, underlining the requirement for a comprehensive methodology that coordinates maintainability into center business techniques.

The fate of oceanic planned operations is being reshaped by progressions in independent advancements, digitalization, and the Web of Things (IoT). Savvy ports, outfitted with computerized cranes, blockchain-based planned operations frameworks, and constant information examination, rethink the limits of effectiveness and network. The consistent joining of data frameworks, robotized processes, and prescient examination upgrades port tasks, decreasing times required to circle back, and improving in general effectiveness. This extraordinary vision stretches out past individual ports to incorporate an interconnected organization of savvy ports that smooth out the whole planned operations chain, from boat to shore.

The ascent of shrewd transportation and interconnected oceanic biological systems presents another component of network protection contemplations. As vessels become progressively dependent on computerized advances, the limits among physical and digital dangers obscure. Network safety turns into a basic part of oceanic tasks, incorporating measures to safeguard vessels, port offices, and the whole store network from digital dangers. The fate of sea online protection rises above customary security standards, requiring vigorous structures, joint effort, and persistent advancement to defend the business against developing digital dangers.

The idea of versatility arises as a critical topic later on possibilities of the sea business. Flexibility reaches out past the capacity to endure outer shocks; it envelops versatility, deftness, and a proactive way to deal with difficulties. Environment versatility, for example, includes planning vessels and sea foundation for outrageous climate occasions and ocean level ascent. Functional versatility includes the capacity to adjust to changing business sector elements, international movements, and innovative disturbances. The quest for flexibility reshapes the business' mentality, inciting a change in outlook that recognizes and plans for vulnerabilities on a worldwide scale.

6.1 Speculation on the future of maritime evolution and the potential for even larger, more advanced vessels.

As the sea business keeps on developing, there is a convincing hypothesis about the future that imagines much bigger, further developed vessels pushing the limits of what was once considered conceivable.

This hypothesis stretches out past the ordinary bounds of sea advancement, bringing up issues about the potential for groundbreaking changes in vessel plan, drive frameworks, and the general size of sea goliaths.

The fate of sea development is complicatedly connected with innovative progressions that rethink the capacities of vessels. One area of hypothesis includes the joining of man-made consciousness (computer based intelligence) and independent innovations on a scale that outperforms current executions. The thought of completely independent vessels, fit for exploring the world's seas without human intercession, challenges customary standards of run tasks. The possibility of vessels furnished with cutting edge sensors, AI calculations, and independent route frameworks presents a dream where the job of human groups might be re-imagined or, at times, totally supplanted.

This shift towards independence raises captivating opportunities for vessel plan. Without the requirements of team convenience and conventional navigational spaces, vessel engineers can imagine totally new designs that amplify freight limit, smooth out streamlined features, and improve by and large proficiency. The speculative eventual fate of oceanic development might see the rise of vessel plans that focus on payload limit, energy proficiency, and novel functionalities empowered by cutting edge innovations. The shortfall of group quarters might prompt a revolutionary rethinking of structure shapes, impetus frameworks, and the reconciliation of state of the art materials to enhance execution.

In this speculative future, impetus frameworks are probably going to go through extraordinary changes. While customary motors controlled by petroleum derivatives right now rule the oceans, there is a developing pattern towards option and cleaner energy sources. The future might observer the far and wide reception of hydrogen power modules, high level battery advancements, or even clever energy sources yet to be created. The shift towards green drive frameworks lines up with the business' obligation to natural maintainability and diminishing ozone harming substance discharges.

Moreover, progressions in materials science are probably going to assume a significant part in forming the fate of oceanic development. The reconciliation of lightweight yet vigorous materials, for example, high level composites or cutting edge compounds, holds the possibility to alter vessel development. These materials add to upgraded eco-friendliness as well as empower the development of bigger vessels without compromising underlying uprightness. The speculative future may grandstand vessels that push the limits of size while keeping an emphasis on natural cognizance.

The rising interest for manageable practices inside the oceanic business is a main thrust behind the hypothesis about the eventual fate of vessel plan. The idea of round economy standards, underscoring reusing, reuse, and negligible waste, could impact how vessels are developed and decommissioned.

In a theoretical situation, vessels planned in light of round economy standards might have measured parts, effectively replaceable parts, and materials that loan themselves to proficient reusing processes. This ground breaking way to deal with maintainability broadens the vessel's lifecycle, lessens ecological effect, and lines up with the business' obligation to capable practices.

One more feature representing things to come of oceanic development includes the investigation of novel advances for impetus and energy age. Hypothesis frequently bases on ideas, for example, sail-helped impetus, using progressed sail plans, or bridling wind and sunlight based ability to enhance conventional drive frameworks. These eco-accommodating advancements, while still in their beginning phases, present energizing opportunities for diminishing dependence on customary powers and bringing down discharges. The speculative future might observer vessels embellished with inventive sails, rotor sails, or even deployable sunlight based chargers, exhibiting an agreeable incorporation of nature's powers into sea tasks.

The improvement of advanced vessels isn't exclusively restricted to freight transporters or holder ships. Traveler vessels, luxury ships, and extravagance yachts are additionally subjects of hypothesis in regards to their future advancement. The voyage business, specifically, may see a change in outlook towards manageability, with vessels intended to limit their natural effect. The coordination of green innovations, energy-proficient frameworks, and high level waste administration arrangements could reclassify the journey insight while lining up with the developing interest for mindful the travel industry.

In the speculative future, the sea business may likewise observe the development of vessels intended for explicit purposes, pushing the limits of specialization. Investigation vessels furnished with best in class innovation for remote ocean research, mining vessels equipped for separating assets from the sea depths, or drifting stages devoted to sustainable power age are inside the domain of plausibility. These profoundly particular vessels could address another time of oceanic investigation and asset use, driven by progressions in mechanical technology, remote detecting, and supportable practices.

The potential for considerably bigger vessels in the speculative future brings up issues about the foundation expected to help them. Ports and terminals might have to go through critical changes to oblige vessels of phenomenal size. The improvement of uber ports furnished with cutting edge stacking and dumping frameworks, computerized cranes, and smoothed out planned operations could turn into a need. The speculative future prompts contemplations about the actual vessels as well as about the whole oceanic biological system, including the foundation, administrative structures, and labor force preparing expected to help the up and coming age of sea monsters.

International contemplations likewise become an integral factor while guessing about the fate of oceanic development. The kickoff of new transportation courses, driven by liquefying ice in the Cold or the improvement of the Northern Ocean Course, could reshape worldwide exchange elements. The speculative future might observer a reconfiguration of sea shipping lanes, with suggestions for the international overall influence, financial organizations, and key coalitions. The potential for expanded sea movement in beforehand out of reach locales presents a layer of intricacy that stretches out past mechanical development.

The speculative eventual fate of oceanic development isn't without difficulties and contemplations. Natural maintainability, administrative structures, international solidness, and the moral ramifications of arising advancements all add to the intricacy of imagining the sea business' future. Finding some kind of harmony among development and obligation is urgent to guarantee that the speculative dreams line up with more extensive cultural objectives, natural safeguarding, and moral principles.

The hypothesis about the fate of oceanic development and the potential for significantly bigger, further developed vessels opens a window into a range of potential outcomes that rise above ebb and flow limits. The intermingling of independence, supportable practices, high level materials, and novel drive frameworks portrays a sea industry that isn't simply developing yet changing. While certain parts of this speculative future might be nearer to acknowledgment than others, the overall subject is one of consistent development, versatility, and a guarantee to forming an oceanic scene that goes past the restrictions of the present creative mind. The eventual fate of sea development is an advancing account, formed by the exchange of innovation, ecological awareness, and the aggregate yearnings of an industry that sails towards unknown skylines.

6.2 Exploration of emerging technologies, including automation, artificial intelligence, and alternative fuels.

The sea business remains at the bleeding edge of an innovative transformation, with arising innovations reshaping the scene of sea tasks. This investigation dives into three critical regions — robotization, man-made consciousness (artificial intelligence), and elective energizes — that are driving advancement, proficiency, and supportability in the sea area.

Mechanization has arisen as an extraordinary power in oceanic tasks, offering the possibility to smooth out processes, improve wellbeing, and upgrade productivity. One eminent use of computerization is in independent vessels, which work without direct human mediation. These automated surface vessels (USVs) influence progressed sensors, AI calculations, and navigational frameworks to independently explore the oceans. The commitment of independent transportation lies in diminished human blunder, expanded functional effectiveness, and upgraded wellbeing.

Past independent vessels, robotization is pervading different parts of oceanic tasks. Robotized cranes at ports, for example, work with productive stacking and dumping of freight, limiting completion times and working on by and large port proficiency. Robotized compartment terminals outfitted with advanced mechanics and transport frameworks empower the consistent development of holders, upgrading efficiency and diminishing work escalated processes. The joining of robotization in sea strategies stretches out to distribution center tasks, stock administration, and store network streamlining, making a more interconnected and productive oceanic biological system.

Computerized reasoning (simulated intelligence) is a significant component in the development of sea innovations, offering the capacity to dissect immense measures of information, go with informed choices, and enhance different cycles. In the domain of route, simulated intelligence driven frameworks add to further developed course arranging, crash evasion, and prescient upkeep. AI calculations, consistently gaining from information inputs, improve the exactness of direction and route, prompting more secure and more proficient oceanic excursions.

Artificial intelligence's effect stretches out past route to eco-friendliness and emanations decrease. Simulated intelligence controlled prescient investigation empower vessel administrators to improve fuel utilization by foreseeing ideal velocities, courses, and motor settings. This lessens fuel costs as well as adds to natural maintainability by bringing down ozone harming substance discharges. The convergence of simulated intelligence and vessel impetus frameworks opens roads for dynamic energy the board, where locally available frameworks adjust progressively to evolving conditions, further streamlining eco-friendliness.

The rise of computerized twins addresses a refined utilization of computer based intelligence in sea tasks. Advanced twins are virtual imitations of actual vessels, consolidating continuous information from sensors and frameworks. These advanced portrayals empower transport administrators to screen, examine, and mimic different situations, working with prescient support, execution improvement, and chance administration. The reconciliation of advanced twins in oceanic tasks represents the extraordinary force of man-made intelligence in making more intelligent, stronger vessels.

Elective fills are at the front line of the sea business' reaction to natural difficulties and administrative prerequisites. Melted petroleum gas (LNG) has acquired conspicuousness as a cleaner-consuming fuel contrasted with conventional marine fills, offering diminished sulfur emanations and lower carbon dioxide (CO_2) yield. LNG-controlled vessels have become progressively predominant, with the advancement of LNG bunkering framework at significant ports supporting the business' change to this elective fuel.

Hydrogen addresses one more boondocks in the mission for maintainable oceanic powers. Hydrogen power devices, which produce power through the response of hydrogen with oxygen, offer a zero-outflow drive arrangement.

While hydrogen-controlled vessels are still in the beginning phases of improvement, progressing exploration and pilot projects are investigating the achievability and adaptability of this innovation. Hydrogen's possible lies in its capacity to act as a perfect and sustainable power hotspot for oceanic drive.

Biofuels got from sustainable sources present a feasible choice for lessening the carbon impression of sea tasks. Biofuels can be delivered from different feedstocks, including green growth, squander materials, and farming buildups. These manageable fills offer a pathway to lessen reliance on petroleum products and add to the business' obligation to harmless to the ecosystem rehearses. Progressing headways in biofuel advancements and expanded creation limits are driving their reception as a standard option in the oceanic area.

Notwithstanding these elective powers, wind-helped impetus frameworks are building up some momentum as a way to saddle environmentally friendly power for oceanic excursions. Rotor sails and kite sails are instances of wind-helped innovations that use wind ability to enhance conventional impetus frameworks. These frameworks have exhibited huge fuel investment funds during long journeys, adding to the business' endeavors to use reasonable energy sources and diminish its natural effect.

The investigation of elective fills is intently attached to the Worldwide Oceanic Association's (IMO) guidelines pointed toward lessening ozone harming substance (GHG) outflows from delivery. The IMO's objectives and rules give a system to the sea business to change towards cleaner and more supportable fills. As the business explores the way towards decarbonization, elective energizes assume a urgent part in gathering emanation decrease objectives and lining up with worldwide endeavors to battle environmental change.

Digitalization, the joining of computerized advancements into different parts of sea activities, fills in as an overall empowering agent for the reception and enhancement of arising advancements. The Web of Things (IoT) interfaces sensors, gadgets, and frameworks installed vessels, making an organization that empowers continuous checking, information assortment, and correspondence. This interconnected environment improves situational mindfulness, upholds prescient upkeep, and works with information driven independent direction.

The execution of computerized twins, as referenced prior, epitomizes the capability of digitalization in making virtual portrayals of actual vessels. These computerized imitations empower remote checking, execution investigation, and situation reenactments, adding to improved functional proficiency and diminished margin time. The information produced by computerized twins feed into man-made intelligence calculations, making an input circle that persistently further develops dynamic cycles and by and large vessel execution.

Blockchain innovation is making advances into oceanic coordinated operations, offering straightforwardness, security, and effectiveness in store network the executives. The decentralized and alter safe nature of blockchain guarantees the honesty of value-based information, lessening the gamble of misrepresentation and improving trust among partners. Shrewd agreements, self-executing contracts with predefined manages, computerize and smooth out legally binding cycles, further advancing strategies tasks.

The execution of independent delivery, described by automated surface vessels (USVs) or independent boats, addresses an extraordinary stage in sea development. Independent vessels influence simulated intelligence, sensors, and navigational advances to work without direct human intercession. The potential advantages incorporate better wellbeing, upgraded functional productivity, and diminished ecological effect through enhanced course arranging and energy-proficient tasks.

The coordination of independent advances reaches out past vessels to incorporate automated ethereal vehicles (UAVs) or drones. Drones furnished with sensors and cameras give ongoing observation of oceanic regions, supporting undertakings like pursuit and salvage, ecological checking, and security. The utilization of robots upgrades situational mindfulness and adds to additional powerful and convenient reactions to oceanic difficulties.

Notwithstanding the promising capability of arising advancements, their far reaching reception faces difficulties and contemplations. Network safety arises as a basic viewpoint, with the rising dependence on computerized frameworks and availability conveying vessels powerless against digital intimidations. The sea business should focus on powerful network safety measures to defend vessels, installed frameworks, and basic foundation from potential cyberattacks.

Administrative structures assume a pivotal part in forming the direction of arising innovations in the sea area. The Worldwide Oceanic Association (IMO) and other administrative bodies set norms and rules to guarantee the protected and mindful combination of advancements like independent delivery, elective powers, and digitalization. The harmonization of guidelines across wards is fundamental to establish a helpful climate for development while keeping an emphasis on security and natural manageability.

Social and labor force contemplations likewise impact the reception of arising advances in the oceanic business. The progress to independent delivery, for instance, brings up issues about the effect on business, preparing necessities for faculty, and the general transformation of the labor force to innovative changes. Industry partners should explore these contemplations and guarantee a smooth progress that boosts the advantages of arising innovations while tending to the human component of oceanic tasks.

The cooperation and commitment of partners across the sea biological system are urgent in cultivating the fruitful execution of arising advances. Industry organizations, research coordinated efforts, and information sharing drives work with the trading of best practices, innovative headways, and illustrations learned. The oceanic local area's aggregate exertion is vital for address normal difficulties, advance development, and drive the business towards a future described by mechanical greatness and supportability.

6.3 Discussion on the implications of evolving maritime trends for global trade and exploration.

The advancing patterns in the oceanic business use significant ramifications for worldwide exchange and investigation, molding the elements of global trade and the limits of sea investigation. This conversation unfurls across a few key aspects, including the effect of mechanical headways, the reconfiguration of worldwide shipping lanes, the job of ecological maintainability, and the international contemplations that highlight the groundbreaking idea of sea patterns.

Mechanical progressions in the oceanic area are introducing another period of proficiency, wellbeing, and availability, generally modifying the scene of worldwide exchange and investigation. The reconciliation of computerization, man-made brainpower, and digitalization is advancing oceanic tasks, from route and operations to vessel the board and port exercises.

The coming of independent delivery stands apart as a unique advantage in the domain of oceanic patterns. Automated surface vessels (USVs) outfitted with cutting edge sensors and independent route frameworks are reclassifying the idea of vessel tasks. The ramifications for worldwide exchange are sweeping, with the potential for diminished functional expenses, upgraded security, and expanded productivity in freight transportation. Independent vessels can work persistently, advancing courses and limiting personal time, subsequently changing the customary elements of delivery plans.

The digitalization of oceanic activities, worked with by the Web of Things (IoT) and information examination, adds to continuous observing, prescient support, and further developed independent direction. The interconnected biological system of sensors and gadgets installed vessels makes an abundance of information that can be utilized to upgrade proficiency and wellbeing. This computerized change reaches out to port tasks, strategies, and store network the executives, making a consistent progression of data across the whole sea organization.

The ramifications of these innovative headways on worldwide exchange are diverse. The decrease of travel times, further developed freight taking care of, and improved consistency in transportation plans reinforce the proficiency of global shipping lanes.

The coordination of advanced advancements in ports empowers quicker and more precise handling of freight, lessening blockage and postponements. Thus, the general seriousness and versatility of worldwide inventory chains are fortified, adding to the assistance of cross-line exchange.

With regards to investigation, mechanical headways open new wildernesses for logical exploration, asset revelation, and marine preservation. Independent submerged vehicles (AUVs) outfitted with cutting edge sensors and imaging advances empower analysts to investigate the profundities of the sea with remarkable accuracy. These vehicles add to the planning of the seabed, the investigation of marine biological systems, and the recognizable proof of important assets.

The ramifications of innovative headways likewise reach out to the ecological manageability of sea exercises. The oceanic business is a critical supporter of worldwide outflows, and the quest for harmless to the ecosystem rehearses has turned into a fundamental concern. Elective powers, energy-proficient advances, and the reception of clean drive frameworks are reclassifying the ecological impression of the sea area.

The shift towards elective energizes, like condensed petroleum gas (LNG) and hydrogen, holds suggestions for worldwide exchange and investigation. LNG-controlled vessels, with lower sulfur emanations and diminished ozone harming substance yield, are turning out to be progressively common. This progress lines up with global guidelines, like the Worldwide Sea Association's (IMO) sulfur cap, which commands the decrease of sulfur discharges from oceanic powers.

Hydrogen, as a perfect and environmentally friendly power source, presents a promising road for manageable oceanic drive. Hydrogen energy components, when incorporated into vessels, offer a zero-outflow arrangement that tends to the basic to decarbonize the sea business. The ramifications of embracing hydrogen as a sea fuel stretch out past emanations decrease; they mean a promise to a greener and more economical future for worldwide exchange and investigation.

Besides, the combination of environmentally friendly power sources, for example, wind-helped impetus frameworks, exhibits a change in outlook in the sea business' way to deal with manageability. Rotor sails, kite sails, and sunlight based chargers on vessels add to diminishing dependence on regular fills and bridling the force of nature for drive. The ramifications of embracing sustainable power in oceanic tasks reach out to a more extensive obligation to relieving the business' effect on the climate.

The ramifications of these supportability patterns on worldwide exchange are critical. As the world moves towards a low-carbon economy, customers and organizations are progressively focusing on maintainability in their store network choices.

The reception of harmless to the ecosystem rehearses in the sea area lines up with these assumptions, impacting the selections of transporters, makers, and coordinated factors suppliers. Supportable transportation rehearses are not only an administrative prerequisite; they enjoy become a cutthroat benefit in the worldwide commercial center.

In the domain of investigation, the coordination of manageable advancements adds to the safeguarding of marine biological systems and the capable use of sea assets. The capacity to direct investigation exercises with insignificant ecological effect upgrades the business' social permit to work and encourages a harmony among investigation and protection.

The reconfiguration of worldwide shipping lanes is one more striking component of developing oceanic patterns. Customarily, significant shipping lanes have been portrayed by deep rooted ways, for example, the Suez Channel, the Panama Trench, and key sea chokepoints. Nonetheless, moving international elements, ecological contemplations, and innovative progressions are affecting the recalibration of these courses.

The launch of new Icy delivery courses, worked with by liquefying ice in the area, has suggestions for worldwide exchange and investigation. The Northern Ocean Course, crossing the Icy waters, offers a more straightforward way among Asia and Europe, possibly lessening travel times and fuel utilization. The ramifications of Icy courses reach out past exchange proficiency; they acquaint new difficulties related with natural protection, vessel wellbeing, and the economical advancement of Cold assets.

The Belt and Street Drive (BRI), drove by China, addresses a groundbreaking power in the reconfiguration of worldwide shipping lanes. The BRI includes the improvement of framework projects, including ports, rail routes, and expressways, to upgrade availability across Asia, Europe, and Africa. The oceanic ramifications of the BRI are clear in the extension of port offices, the improvement of sea passages, and the expanded sea exchange between taking part countries.

The ramifications of these changes in worldwide shipping lanes reach out to the international scene. Vital contemplations, monetary partnerships, and the journey for international impact shape the turn of events and use of oceanic courses. Countries decisively position themselves to tie down admittance to key oceanic chokepoints, control imperative ocean paths, and partake in arising exchange passages. The international ramifications highlight the interconnectedness of sea patterns with more extensive international contemplations.

The South China Ocean, a critical sea district, embodies the international ramifications of developing sea patterns. Disagreements about regional cases, route privileges, and asset investigation in the South China Ocean have suggestions for worldwide exchange, provincial strength, and global relations.

The essential significance of sea regions and their possible effect on shipping lanes highlights the complicated exchange between sea patterns and international contemplations.

The investigation of new wildernesses, worked with by advancing sea advancements, acquaints contemplations related with sway, asset the board, and worldwide cooperation. As countries investigate the seabed for important assets, for example, minerals and interesting earth components, questions emerge about the impartial circulation of advantages, natural stewardship, and adherence to worldwide guidelines. The ramifications of investigation stretch out past logical disclosure to the mindful and feasible usage of marine assets.

Ecological manageability arises as a characterizing factor in the ramifications of developing oceanic patterns. The sea business, perceiving its job in natural stewardship, is going through a change in perspective towards greener practices. The ramifications of supportability patterns stretch out to administrative consistence, shopper inclinations, and the business' social obligation.

Administrative structures, like the Global Oceanic Association's (IMO) guidelines on sulfur emanations and ozone depleting substance decrease, shape the natural ramifications of sea exercises. The reception of these guidelines impacts vessel configuration, fuel decisions, and functional practices. The ramifications of administrative consistence reach out to the business' standing, monetary suitability, and arrangement with worldwide endeavors to address environmental change.

Buyer inclinations and corporate obligation assume a crucial part in molding the ramifications of maintainability patterns. As natural mindfulness develops among buyers, there is a rising interest for items and administrations that stick to economical and moral practices. The sea business, as a basic part of worldwide stockpile chains, isn't safe to these inclinations. Transporters, producers, and planned operations suppliers are investigating the supportability practices of oceanic accomplices, affecting choices about freight transportation and coordinated factors.

The ramifications of manageability drifts likewise stretch out to monetary contemplations inside the sea business. Interests in cleaner advancements, elective energizes, and energy-productive vessels have suggestions for the business' capital use, functional expenses, and long haul monetary maintainability. The progress towards supportability requires an essential methodology that offsets financial feasibility with ecological obligation.

Social obligation inside the oceanic business incorporates contemplations connected with the prosperity of sea networks, the wellbeing of sailors, and the effect of sea exercises on beach front biological systems. The ramifications of supportability patterns on friendly obligation incorporate endeavors to limit the business' effect on marine conditions, moderate the impacts of oceanic mishaps, and add to the prosperity of networks that rely upon sea exercises.

The job of the oceanic business in accomplishing more extensive supportability objectives, like the Unified Countries Manageable Improvement Objectives (SDGs), highlights the interconnectedness of natural, social, and monetary ramifications. The sea area's obligation to supportability is fundamental to addressing worldwide difficulties connected with environmental change, biodiversity protection, and capable asset usage.

Chapter 7

Navigating the Unknown

Exploring the obscure is a significant excursion that rises above the simple demonstration of navigating strange waters; it typifies the substance of investigation, disclosure, and the unstoppable human soul. This campaign into the obscure is meaningful of the sea business' nonstop journey to push limits, conquer difficulties, and open the secrets that lie underneath the outer layer of immense seas. In this investigation, we dive into the multi-layered elements of exploring the obscure, enveloping the verifiable, mechanical, ecological, and optimistic aspects that characterize this remarkable journey.

At its center, exploring the obscure exemplifies the authentic account of oceanic investigation that traverses hundreds of years. From the brave excursions of early sailors who actually considered cruising past the known skylines to the period of disclosure that revealed new mainlands, the sea business has been at the front line of human investigation. The stories of sailors like Christopher Columbus, Ferdinand Magellan, and Zheng He encapsulate the daringness to cruise into the obscure, directed by divine route, simple guides, and an enduring assurance to disentangle the secrets of neglected domains.

The coming of oceanic shipping lanes, associating far off corners of the globe, established the groundwork for social trade, financial flourishing, and the globalization of civilizations. The Silk Street, the zest courses, and the three-sided shipping lanes mirror the interconnectedness encouraged by oceanic investigation. These verifiable undertakings, driven by the quest for riches, information, and experience, have made a permanent imprint on the texture of mankind's set of experiences, profoundly shaping social orders, economies, and the actual forms of the world guide.

In the cutting edge period, the soul of exploring the obscure has developed close by mechanical advancements that rethink the abilities of oceanic investigation. The progress from sail to steam, the improvement of cutting edge route instruments, and the presentation of sonar and radar innovations have reformed the manner in which sailors explore strange waters. Satellite-based situating frameworks, like GPS, give uncommon exactness in deciding a vessel's area, empowering protected and proficient route even in the most remote pieces of the seas.

Subs and remotely worked vehicles (ROVs) address innovative wonders that expand the limits of submerged investigation. These high level vehicles, furnished with refined sensors and cameras, dive into the profundities of the sea, disclosing biological systems, land elements, and marine life that were once covered in secret. The capacity to explore the obscure submerged domains, from the deep fields to remote ocean channels, opens roads for logical revelation, asset investigation, and ecological preservation.

Exploring the obscure isn't without its difficulties, and the sea business has experienced and defeated various hindrances as its continued looking for investigation. Slippery atmospheric conditions, flighty flows, and the tremendousness of the vast ocean present impressive difficulties that sailors go up against with ability, experience, and mechanical ability. The dangers of exploring through ice-plagued waters, storm inclined areas, or clogged oceanic chokepoints highlight the strength and versatility expected to explore the unexplored world.

Ecological contemplations have become progressively indispensable to the account of exploring the unexplored world. The effect of human exercises on marine biological systems, the results of environmental change on ocean levels and weather conditions, and the conservation of biodiversity in neglected locales request a faithful way to deal with sea investigation. The business' obligation to supportable practices, marine protection, and the moderation of natural effect mirrors a change in perspective in exploring the obscure with an awareness of certain expectations and environmental care.

In the contemporary setting, exploring the obscure reaches out past actual investigation to the domains of digitalization, information examination, and man-made reasoning. The sea business is at the front line of utilizing state of the art advances to improve route, enhance functional proficiency, and guarantee the security of vessels.

Prescient investigation, AI calculations, and ongoing information handling engage sailors with bits of knowledge that add to better navigation, risk the executives, and the general viability of sea activities.

The obscure, in the advanced period, incorporates the immense scope of oceanic information that holds the way to opening functional efficiencies and key experiences. The joining of the Web of Things (IoT) into sea frameworks interfaces sensors, gadgets, and installed frameworks, making an organization that produces a consistent stream of information. This information driven way to deal with route empowers condition-based upkeep, fuel streamlining, and a proactive reaction to arising difficulties, changing the manner in which vessels explore through the intricacies of current sea tasks.

The ramifications of computerized route reach out to the idea of independent delivery, where vessels explore without direct human mediation. Independent surface vessels (ASVs) furnished with man-made consciousness, sensors, and high level route frameworks address a wilderness in exploring the unexplored world. The potential advantages incorporate expanded wellbeing, diminished human mistake, and improved functional proficiency. Be that as it may, the reception of independent delivery additionally raises contemplations connected with administrative systems, network protection, and the human component in oceanic tasks.

Exploring the obscure, in the advanced age, includes getting basic oceanic framework against digital dangers. The interconnected idea of oceanic frameworks, dependence on computerized advances, and the mix of independent abilities make weaknesses that require powerful network protection measures. The ramifications of network safety in exploring the obscure reach out past the security of vessels to envelop the shielding of delicate oceanic information, guaranteeing the honesty of route frameworks, and maintaining the strength of the whole sea environment.

International contemplations add a layer of intricacy to the story of exploring the unexplored world. The essential significance of oceanic domains, challenged waters, and the journey for asset rich districts impact worldwide relations, monetary coalitions, and international strains. The South China Ocean, for instance, epitomizes the international ramifications of exploring the obscure, as regional debates, contending claims, and the essential situating of maritime resources make a complex sea scene with worldwide implications.

The kickoff of new Icy transportation courses, driven by softening ice in the locale, presents international contemplations in exploring already difficult to reach waters. The potential for abbreviated travel times, asset investigation, and monetary open doors in the Icy district draws in the consideration of Icy and non-Icy countries the same. The ramifications of exploring the Cold reach out to issues of sway, natural conservation, and the advancement of administrative systems to administer the practical utilization of this extraordinary and delicate environment.

The quest for exploring the obscure is additionally entwined with desires for space investigation. The sea business assumes a urgent part in supporting space dispatches, with oceanic stages filling in as platforms, recuperation zones, and transportation center points for space-related exercises. The ramifications of this union among oceanic and space investigation reach out to mechanical headways, global joint effort, and the rise of spaceports adrift, mirroring humankind's journey to investigate wildernesses past our home planet.

Yearnings for exploring the obscure incorporate the mission for extraterrestrial assets, with space rocks and divine bodies becoming likely supplies of important minerals. The convergence of oceanic and space investigation acquaints contemplations related with the legitimate structures administering space exercises, the mindful use of room assets, and the potential for coordinated effort among sea and space ventures in molding the eventual fate of interplanetary investigation.

The obscure, in the sea setting, likewise envelops the investigation of remote ocean environments and the secrets disguised in the sea profundities. Aqueous vents, submerged mountains, and unfamiliar ocean bottom natural surroundings harbor special living things and land includes that remain to a great extent neglected. The ramifications of exploring the obscure in remote ocean investigation reach out to logical disclosure, the comprehension of marine biodiversity, and the potential for biotechnological developments got from remote ocean organic entities.

In exploring the obscure, the sea business embraces a forward-looking point of view that stretches out past prompt difficulties to long haul manageability. The business' obligation to natural stewardship, administrative consistence, and the reception of green innovations mirrors a shared mindset about the effect of oceanic exercises in the world. The ramifications of this manageability outlook include consistence with existing guidelines as well as proactive endeavors to surpass natural norms, lessen outflows, and add to worldwide endeavors to address environmental change.

The cooperative idea of exploring the obscure is obvious in global drives that unite countries, ventures, and established researchers chasing shared objectives. The Unified Countries Show on the Law of the Ocean (UNCLOS) gives a system to participation, asset the executives, and the tranquil goal of sea debates. Provincial arrangements, research organizations, and information sharing drives add to an aggregate exertion in exploring the obscure with a feeling of coordinated effort and shared liability.

7.1 Reflection on the overall impact of giants of maritime evolution on human society and the global economy.

The monsters of oceanic development, giant ships that exemplify the zenith of designing and mechanical ability, significantly affect human culture and the world-wide economy.

This reflection looks to dive into the multi-layered components of this effect, investigating how these sea behemoths have molded exchange, interconnected countries, worked with financial development, and added to the texture of human progress.

At the core of the conversation lies the job of these sea monsters in changing worldwide exchange. These mammoth vessels, with their monstrous freight limits and productivity, have turned into the key part of global trade. The advancement from humble freight boats to the present super holder transporters has changed the operations scene, considering the transportation of merchandise on an uncommon scale.

The containerization transformation, a critical part of sea development, has smoothed out the method involved with stacking, dumping, and shipping merchandise across seas. Normalized holders, effectively adaptable between boats, trucks, and trains, have turned into the structure blocks of a consistently coordinated worldwide inventory network. This normalization has sped up the development of products as well as diminished costs, limited blunders, and improved the general productivity of sea coordinated factors.

The effect of these oceanic goliaths on exchange isn't bound to productivity gains alone. The sheer size of their freight conveying abilities has worked with the globalization of ventures. Fabricating focuses can now be decisively found, exploiting practical creation, while depending on these gigantic vessels to move products to shoppers all over the planet productively. This has prompted the scattering of supply chains and the making of perplexing organizations that range landmasses.

The interconnectivity worked with by oceanic monsters has led to a really worldwide economy. Natural substances from one corner of the world can consistently track down their approach to assembling centers, where they are changed into completed products, just to be appropriated universally. The monsters of sea development, as the veins of this worldwide monetary circulatory framework, have considered the specialization of locales, cultivating financial reliance and making a dynamic where the thriving of one country is complicatedly connected to the prosperity of others.

Besides, the advancement of oceanic innovation has catalyzed the development of specific businesses, especially in shipbuilding and related sea administrations. Countries with strong shipbuilding capacities have situated themselves as central participants in the worldwide oceanic industry, contributing altogether to their economies. The interest for progressively complex vessels has prodded development in transport plan, impetus frameworks, and route innovations, making an expanding influence of monetary development in related areas.

The effect of sea advancement stretches out past financial contemplations to international elements. Command over sea courses and the capacity to explore decisively significant streams have forever been critical components in the international chessboard.

Countries with admittance to and impact over key oceanic chokepoints, for example, the Panama Waterway, the Suez Trench, and the Waterway of Malacca, hold critical international influence.

Besides, the rise of new Cold delivery courses because of softening ice has acquainted another aspect with international contemplations. The Icy, when a difficult to reach boondocks, is currently turning into a reasonable option for specific transportation courses. The ramifications of these improvements are monetary as well as international, as countries position themselves to attest impact in the Icy locale and explore the intricacies of asset investigation, regional cases, and natural protection.

Ecological contemplations have become progressively key to the talk on the effect of monsters of oceanic advancement. The size of these vessels, combined with the sheer volume of oceanic traffic, has raised worries about the environmental impression of the sea business. The consuming of non-renewable energy sources, outflows of ozone harming substances, and the gamble of oil slicks present huge ecological difficulties.

Accordingly, there is a developing accentuation on manageability inside the oceanic area. The turn of events and reception of cleaner drive advancements, elective energizes, and energy-effective practices are reshaping the business' way to deal with ecological stewardship. The effect of these supportability drives stretches out past consistence with guidelines; it addresses a more extensive obligation to relieving the natural effect of oceanic exercises and lining up with worldwide endeavors to battle environmental change.

The goliaths of oceanic development have likewise assumed a vital part in forming metropolitan scenes and the improvement of port urban communities. Ports, when unobtrusive harbors, have changed into rambling edifices with cutting edge framework to oblige the consistently expanding size of vessels. The financial energy of these port urban areas is interwoven with the recurring pattern of sea exchange, making center points of business, industry, and social trade.

The effect of oceanic advancement on port urban areas stretches out past the actual framework to the social and social texture of these networks. Ports, generally entryways to the world, have been mixtures of societies, encouraging variety and cosmopolitanism. The sea business, with its huge organization of exchange and correspondence, has been an impetus for the trading of thoughts, customs, and developments, molding the social personality of port urban communities.

The monetary effect of oceanic monsters isn't restricted to the seaside districts alone. Inland transportation organizations, including rail lines and thruways, are fundamentally associated with sea shipping lanes.

The advancement of productive multi-purpose transportation frameworks guarantees the consistent development of merchandise from ports to inland objections as well as the other way around. This network broadens the financial effect of oceanic advancement to landlocked areas, making passages of monetary action that transmit from significant ports.

The effect of oceanic advancement on human culture goes past substantial financial and infrastructural transforms; it envelops immaterial components like training, development, and the quest for information. The oceanic business has been a cauldron for mastering and ability improvement, encouraging a labor force with particular skill in route, designing, coordinated factors, and sea regulation. Oceanic instruction foundations, research focuses, and preparing offices have thrived, adding to the development of an educated and talented labor force.

Development inside the oceanic area has been a main thrust behind the advancement of vessels and functional practices. The mission for proficiency, security, and natural manageability has prompted headways in transport plan, drive advancements, and route frameworks. The effect of these advancements stretches out past the oceanic business to impact more extensive mechanical patterns, motivating improvements in regions like computerization, man-made consciousness, and clean energy.

The effect of oceanic development on human culture additionally envelops the difficulties and dangers intrinsic in sea exercises. Mishaps, oil slicks, and ecological calamities have highlighted the requirement for rigid wellbeing guidelines and crisis reaction systems. The illustrations gained from sea occurrences add to the consistent improvement of security guidelines, preparing conventions, and chance alleviation systems, guaranteeing that the effect of oceanic exercises on human culture stays positive and maintainable.

The social effect of sea development is reflected in workmanship, writing, and the aggregate creative mind of social orders. Sea subjects pervade writing, from exemplary stories of ocean journeys to contemporary accounts that investigate the human experience on the high oceans. Imaginative articulations, including works of art, figures, and sea exhibition halls, give recognition to the magnificence of sea investigation and the persevering through charm of the vast ocean.

The effect of monsters of oceanic development on worldwide exchange and investigation, when seen from the perspective of human culture, is an embroidery woven with strings of monetary reliance, social trade, mechanical development, and ecological obligation. The sea business, with its monsters exploring the world's seas, has turned into a representation for human flexibility, versatility, and the quest for progress. As we consider this effect, we perceive that the monsters of oceanic advancement have not just formed the course of worldwide exchange and investigation however have additionally made a permanent imprint on the human story, helping us to remember the perplexing connection among mankind and the immense span of the world's oceans.

7.2 Contemplation of the ongoing challenges and opportunities in the world of large ships.

The examination of the continuous difficulties and open doors in the realm of huge boats uncovers a perplexing and dynamic scene formed by a horde of elements. These huge vessels, frequently alluded to as the monsters of the oceans, face a range of provokes going from mechanical progressions to ecological maintainability, while simultaneously introducing open doors for development, monetary development, and worldwide network.

At the cutting edge of the difficulties is the determined quest for mechanical progressions in transport plan and activity. The universe of huge boats is seeing an extraordinary period set apart by the reconciliation of computerized innovations, robotization, and man-made brainpower. While these developments hold the commitment of upgrading productivity, wellbeing, and route capacities, they likewise present difficulties as far as execution costs, administrative systems, and the requirement for a talented labor force fit for exploring this new innovative boondocks.

The coming of independent transportation, a huge innovative turn of events, presents the two difficulties and valuable open doors. The possibility of automated vessels exploring the oceans brings up issues about administrative systems, wellbeing conventions, and the human component in sea tasks. Challenges remember the requirement for global agreement for independent transportation norms, network safety concerns, and tending to the likely effect on work inside the oceanic business. Notwithstanding, the open doors lie in the potential for expanded security, functional proficiency, and cost-adequacy, as well as the capacity to explore risky circumstances without presenting human teams to chances.

Ecological manageability stands apart as a fundamental test in the domain of huge boats. The natural impression of these vessels, described by emanations of ozone depleting substances, air poisons, and the gamble of oil slicks, has incited an increased spotlight on moderating ecological effect. The sea business is under expanding strain to embrace cleaner impetus innovations, elective energizes, and energy-proficient practices. Nonetheless, the test lies in mechanical arrangements as well as in the turn of events and implementation of worldwide guidelines that advance manageable practices across the whole lifecycle of enormous boats.

The basic to diminish outflows has led to developments like melted flammable gas (LNG) impetus, hydrogen power modules, and wind-helped drive frameworks. While these innovations offer a pathway towards greener delivery, challenges continue concerning foundation improvement, the accessibility of elective fills, and the monetary reasonability of progressing from traditional energizes. The oceanic business wrestles with the need to offset ecological contemplations with the reasonable items of vessel activity and financial supportability.

One more test in the realm of enormous boats rotates around the intricacies of sea network safety. As vessels become progressively associated through advanced networks and dependent on mechanization, the weakness to digital dangers develops. The potential dangers incorporate information breaks, situation controls, and the split the difference of route and correspondence frameworks. Shielding oceanic foundation from digital dangers requests not just innovative arrangements like hearty network protection systems and conventions yet in addition a proactive way to deal with network protection schooling and preparing inside the sea labor force.

International elements add a layer of intricacy to the difficulties looked by huge boats. The sea business works inside an international scene impacted by regional questions, exchange strains, and developing worldwide relations. The essential meaning of sea chokepoints, like the Waterway of Hormuz and the South China Ocean, acquaints vulnerabilities related with navigational opportunity, security, and the potential for international struggles that could upset sea shipping lanes.

The continuous difficulties, in any case, coincide with a range of chances that characterize the universe of huge boats. One of the unmistakable open doors lies in the persistent quest for mechanical development. The incorporation of computerized advancements, information investigation, and man-made brainpower holds the possibility to reform sea tasks. From prescient upkeep and constant observing to independent route and savvy port administration, these developments can upgrade productivity, diminish functional expenses, and add to the general intensity of the oceanic business.

The digitalization of oceanic tasks stretches out to the idea of the savvy transport, where best in class sensors, network, and computerization combine to make vessels equipped for ideal execution and continuous direction. Shrewd boats offer open doors for further developed route, eco-friendliness, and wellbeing through the mix of cutting edge innovations like Web of Things (IoT) gadgets, AI calculations, and network arrangements that empower consistent correspondence among boats and shore-based frameworks.

The approach of huge information examination in the sea business opens open doors for prescient support, execution enhancement, and information driven direction. By tackling the abundance of information created by huge boats, administrators can proactively address possible issues, upgrade fuel utilization, and improve generally functional productivity. This information driven approach works on the unwavering quality of vessel tasks as well as adds to the advancement of more astute and more maintainable oceanic practices.

The quest for elective powers and impetus frameworks addresses one more road of chance in the realm of huge boats. As the business wrestles with the ecological test of decreasing emanations, the investigation of cleaner energy sources picks up speed.

Melted gaseous petrol (LNG), thought about a momentary fuel, is progressively being embraced as an all the more harmless to the ecosystem option in contrast to customary marine fills. Additionally, continuous innovative work in hydrogen power devices, alkali, and biofuels present promising open doors for accomplishing zero-emanation delivering from now on.

The execution of wind-helped impetus frameworks, for example, rotor sails and kite sails, features a renaissance old enough old innovations adjusted for current sea needs. These inventive arrangements tackle wind energy to enhance conventional impetus, offering open doors for fuel investment funds and outflows decrease. The cooperative energy among conventional and state of the art advances embodies the versatility and flexibility of the oceanic business even with ecological difficulties.

The universe of enormous ships likewise presents open doors for monetary development and worldwide availability. The sheer size of these vessels empowers the effective transportation of products across huge distances, interfacing makers and customers on a worldwide scale. As the worldwide populace proceeds to develop and financial exercises become progressively interconnected, the interest for huge boats as the foundation of global exchange is supposed to endure, encouraging monetary turn of events and adding to the flourishing of countries.

The extension of sea shipping lanes, driven by variables like the dissolving of Icy ice, presents potential open doors for new roads of route and asset investigation. The kickoff of Icy courses, albeit joined by ecological difficulties and international contemplations, offers the potential for abbreviated travel times, expanded availability, and the advancement of new monetary passages. This developing sea scene sets out open doors for countries to broaden their shipping lanes, investigate undiscovered assets, and reinforce financial binds with Icy districts.

The reconciliation of supportable practices inside the oceanic business tends to natural difficulties as well as presents open doors for separation and upper hand. The interest for eco-accommodating and socially dependable transportation rehearses is developing among customers, organizations, and administrative bodies. Huge transportation organizations that proactively embrace practical measures, like emanation decrease drives, eco-accommodating vessel plans, and adherence to worldwide natural principles, position themselves as pioneers in the business, drawing in earth cognizant clients and cultivating a positive public picture.

Also, the universe of enormous boats gives open doors to coordinated effort and information trade. Global drives, research organizations, and industry discussions work with the sharing of best practices, mechanical developments, and examples learned.

Cooperative endeavors in regions like natural maintainability, security guidelines, and mechanical headways add to the aggregate versatility and progress of the oceanic business on a worldwide scale.

The examination of the continuous difficulties and open doors in the realm of huge boats uncovers a unique scene portrayed by a fragile harmony between mechanical development, ecological maintainability, international elements, and monetary reliance. The difficulties, going from the combination of state of the art advancements to tending to ecological worries, highlight the intricacy of exploring the oceans in the 21st hundred years. All the while, the potential open doors introduced by mechanical advancement, manageable practices, and worldwide network grandstand the business' versatility and limit with regards to transformation. As the universe of huge boats diagrams its course into the future, the interaction among difficulties and potential open doors will shape the direction of an industry that stays crucial for worldwide exchange, monetary turn of events, and the interconnectedness of countries.

7.3 Closing thoughts on the enduring legacy of these nautical wonders.

In reflecting upon the persevering through tradition of these nautical miracles — epic ships that have explored the oceans, molded worldwide exchange, and typified the pinnacle of sea designing — one can't resist the urge to wonder about the permanent engraving they have left on mankind's set of experiences and the world at large. These sea monsters, with their transcending bodies and innovative refinement, rise above simple vessels; they stand as landmarks to human creativity, flexibility, and the tenacious journey to vanquish the limitless breadth of the world's seas.

The tradition of these nautical marvels is entwined with the rich embroidered artwork of oceanic history. From the glorious trimmers that once hustled across the oceans in the period of sail to the contemporary uber holder delivers that structure the foundation of worldwide exchange, every time has seen the advancement of sea designing and route. The heritage is, in numerous ways, a continuum — a story of investigation, exchange, and social trade that traverses hundreds of years.

The Period of Investigation, proclaimed by gutsy sailors like Columbus, Magellan, and Zheng He, established the groundwork for the sea inheritance we witness today. These early globe-trotters, pushed by a feeling of interest and the craving to graph neglected regions, set forth into the unexplored world. Their excursions extended the referred to world as well as laid out the sea courses and navigational procedures that would shape ensuing hundreds of years of nautical.

The tradition of sea ponders reaches out to the financial domains of exchange and business. The Silk Street, the zest courses, and the three-sided shipping lanes are waypoints in the verifiable tradition of oceanic exchange. As the interest for products rose above provincial limits, oceanic shipping lanes turned into the courses through which human advancements traded wares, thoughts, and social impacts. The oceanic heritage, in this way, is profoundly entwined with the financial relationship that describes the advanced globalized world.

The modern transformation denoted a crucial section in the sea heritage, presenting mechanical developments that changed the scale and proficiency of oceanic transportation. Steam motors supplanted sails, and iron bodies replaced wooden vessels, introducing a period of exceptional sea progress. The tradition of this mechanical transformation is obvious in the progress from windjammers to steamships, representing the victory of human designing over the constraints of nature.

In the twentieth hundred years, the sea heritage saw the coming of containerization — a change in perspective that upset the coordinated operations of worldwide exchange. Compartment ships, with their normalized freight units, smoothed out the stacking and dumping processes, emphatically lessening times required to circle back in ports and expanding the productivity of sea transportation. This development reshaped supply chains, sped up the speed of business, and added to the financial globalization that portrays the contemporary world.

The tradition of these nautical marvels isn't bound to the financial and authentic domains; it stretches out to the international scene. Command over key oceanic chokepoints, for example, the Panama Channel, the Suez Trench, and the Waterway of Malacca, has been a wellspring of international influence and conflict. The tradition of sea international relations highlights the significance of ocean courses in molding the overall influence, encouraging unions, and impacting worldwide relations.

The persevering through tradition of these nautical miracles is scratched in the social and cultural stories of seaside networks and oceanic countries. Ports, when humble harbors, have developed into clamoring metropolitan focuses, their horizons interspersed by cranes and the poles of holder ships. The heritage is obvious in the sea customs, marine fables, and the social personality of networks whose chronicles are entwined with the recurring pattern of the tides.

Innovative headways, a foundation of the oceanic inheritance, keep on molding the contemporary sea scene. The monsters of the present oceans — super enormous holder ships, oil big haulers, and condensed gaseous petrol transporters — are the exemplifications of state of the art designing. The heritage is apparent in the reception of advanced advancements, computerization, and man-made consciousness that upgrade route, improve eco-friendliness, and add to the general wellbeing of sea tasks.

The tradition of sea ponders stretches out to the ecological cognizance that pervades the business in the 21st hundred years. As the natural effect of sea exercises goes under investigation, the heritage is characterized by a guarantee to reasonable practices. From the improvement of eco-accommodating drive frameworks to the investigation of elective energizes, the oceanic business is effectively looking for arrangements that line up with the objectives of natural stewardship.

In examining the persevering through tradition of these nautical miracles, one should recognize the continuous difficulties that go with their heritage into what's in store. The mission for manageability, typified by the need to diminish emanations and relieve natural effect, remains as a characterizing challenge. The tradition of sea ponders faces the business with the basic to explore the oceans with an uplifted feeling of obligation for the seas and the planet.

The heritage additionally wrestles with the intricacies of international elements and the potential for oceanic struggles. As countries strive for command over essential streams, state sway in challenged districts, and explore the moving sands of worldwide relations, the tradition of oceanic miracles becomes laced with the goals of harmony, strategy, and the dependable work-out of sea power.

The tradition of mechanical development, while offering open doors for proficiency and wellbeing, presents difficulties connected with the human component in oceanic activities. The coming of independent delivery, savvy boats, and digitalization presents inquiries concerning labor force flexibility, preparing necessities, and the expected re-location of customary oceanic jobs. The heritage requests a sensitive harmony between mechanical advancement and the conservation of the human touch in nautical.

As the tradition of these nautical marvels unfurls in the 21st 100 years, it is set apart by a unique transaction of difficulties, open doors, and obligations. The heritage is certainly not a static scene of sea accomplishments however a living story that unfurls with each excursion across the oceans. It is a demonstration of the strength of the sea business, the flexibility of sailors, and the continuous mission to reclassify the limits of sea greatness.

The persevering through tradition of these nautical marvels welcomes examination on the ageless soul of investigation, advancement, and interconnectedness that char-acterizes the oceanic account. The inheritance is a continuum that traverses the ages, from the primary sailors who wandered into the great beyond to the contemporary sailors who explore the world's seas with accuracy and expertise. A heritage entices people in the future to proceed with the sea venture, to diagram new courses, and to maintain the upsides of stewardship, coordinated effort, and a significant regard for the tremendous and mysterious domain of the oceans.

In digging further into the persevering through tradition of these nautical marvels, it becomes obvious that their effect reaches out past the domains of exchange, inno-vation, and international relations. The inheritance is complicatedly woven into the texture of human progress, impacting the commonsense parts of sea exercises as well as penetrating social, creative, and cultural aspects.

The social reverberation of sea ponders is strikingly portrayed in workmanship, writing, and the aggregate creative mind of social orders.

The boundlessness of the untamed ocean, the appeal of far off skylines, and the boldness of mariners have enlivened innumerable works of writing and craftsmanship since forever ago. Sea topics are repetitive in legendary stories of ocean journeys, books portraying life on the high oceans, and imaginative portrayals that catch the greatness and persona of sea investigation.

Sea craftsmanship, going from works of art to figures, fills in as a visual demon-stration of the dazzling idea of these nautical marvels. From famous portrayals of magnificent cruising boats to current translations of contemporary vessels, oceanic craftsmanship catches the embodiment of the sea heritage. Specialists, enlivened by the powerful interaction of ocean and sky, have added to the formation of a visual story that rises above time and addresses the persevering through interest with the sea domain.

Writing, as well, has been a vessel through which the tradition of oceanic marvels has been passed on to progressive ages. Exemplary works, for example, Herman Melville's "Moby-Dick," Joseph Conrad's "Heart of Dimness," and Patrick O'Brian's "Lord and Leader" tell stories of sea undertakings as well as dive into the significant human encounters and existential difficulties looked by the people who adventure into the unexplored world. These scholarly show-stoppers have become necessary parts of the sea inheritance, encapsulating investigation, the fellowship among mariners, and the secrets of the ocean.

The cultural effect of oceanic miracles is apparent in the improvement of waterfront networks and port urban areas. Ports, when humble harbors, have developed into dynamic metropolitan communities that act as doors to the world. The tradition of oceanic exercises is scratched in the framework of these urban areas, from the clamoring moors and quays to the sea historical centers that commend the historical backdrop of nautical. The monetary thriving of these beach front networks is unpredictably connected to the oceanic inheritance, as the appearance and flight of boats shape the rhythms of day to day existence.

The cultural effect isn't bound to beach front areas alone; it broadens inland through the complicated organizations of transportation and exchange. Rail routes, parkways, and interconnected operations frameworks work with the development of products from ports to inland objections, making monetary passages that length mainlands. The tradition of sea ponders, as the corridors of worldwide exchange, emanates into the hinterlands, cultivating monetary action, work creation, and the trading of products and thoughts.

Also, the cultural effect of sea ponders is reflected in the assorted and cosmopolitan nature of oceanic networks. Nautical has generally been a global calling, uniting people from various societies, foundations, and ethnicities. The tradition of sea variety is apparent in the multicultural teams of boats, where mariners from different corners of the globe work together in the common undertaking of exploring the oceans. This social trade, worked with by oceanic exercises, adds to the lavishness and variety of waterfront networks and port urban areas.

The getting through tradition of sea ponders additionally includes the immaterial legacy of sea customs and legends. Marine people group, saturated with a legacy formed by hundreds of years of oceanic exercises, convey forward customs, odd notions, and stories that mirror the difficulties and wins of life adrift. The tradition of sea old stories is an embroidery woven with stories of ocean beasts, phantom boats, and the legend of mariners who have overcame whirlwinds and investigated unknown waters. These stories, went down through ages, add to the social character of sea networks and act as a demonstration of the strength and fortitude of sailors.

Mechanical developments, a foundation of the oceanic inheritance, have changed the pragmatic parts of route as well as impacted cultural ways of behaving and communications. The appearance of steamships in the nineteenth 100 years, for instance, reformed transportation as well as reshaped impression of time and distance. The capacity to navigate seas in a small part of the time recently required united far off lands, cultivating a feeling of interconnectedness and globalization that keeps on characterizing the cutting edge world.

The effect of innovation reaches out to the domain of correspondence, where developments like radio, satellite correspondence, and the web have changed the elements of sea availability. The tradition of oceanic marvels is clear in the immediate correspondence among boats and shore, the constant observing of vessels, and the interconnectedness of a worldwide sea organization. These mechanical headways have upgraded security and functional effectiveness as well as added to a feeling of worldwide local area among sailors and sea partners.

The persevering through tradition of oceanic miracles is additionally highlighted by their job in logical investigation and exploration. Ships, outfitted with cutting edge labs and exploration offices, act as stages for oceanographic studies, sea life science examination, and environment observing. The tradition of sea investigation stretches out past business interests to the quest for information about the seas and their part in molding the planet's environments. The information and experiences earned from sea research add to how we might interpret environmental change, marine biodiversity, and the sensitive equilibrium of the seas.

In mulling over the persevering through tradition of sea ponders, one must likewise recognize the difficulties that continue in the cutting edge time. The effect of sea exercises on the climate, including worries about discharges, oil slicks, and the interruption of marine biological systems, highlights the requirement for economical practices and natural stewardship. The tradition of sea exercises requests a proactive way to deal with tending to these difficulties, consolidating imaginative arrangements, and cultivating a pledge to saving the strength of the seas for people in the future.

The persevering through tradition of sea ponders fills in as a wellspring of motivation for future undertakings in the oceanic space.

As the business keeps on exploring the oceans, it conveys with it the obligation to maintain the upsides of security, natural manageability, and worldwide participation. The inheritance is a directing light, enlightening a way ahead that offsets progress with liability, development with safeguarding, and investigation with stewardship.